Canon EOS M200 User Companion

Your Indispensable Handbook with Illustrations to Master the EOS M200

By

Mats Sauer

Table of Content

3

INTRODUCTION

The Canon EOS M200 is a mirrorless interchangeable-lens camera (MILC) that is perfect for both beginners and experienced photographers alike. It is lightweight and compact, making it easy to carry around with you wherever you go. The M200 also features a variety of easy-to-use features, such as a flip-up touchscreen display and a variety of creative shooting modes.

The Canon EOS M200 features a variety of shooting modes to choose from, each of which is designed for different types of photography. In the second chapter of this user guide, we will cover each of these shooting modes in detail, so that you can learn how to use them to capture the best possible photos.

Welcome to the Canon EOS M200 User Guide! This guide is designed to help you get the most out of your new camera, whether you're a beginner or a seasoned pro.

This user guide will cover everything you need to know about your new Canon EOS M200 camera. From getting to know the basic controls to learning how to take advanced creative photos, we will walk you through it all step-by-step.

Chapter 1: Getting The Camera Up and Running

Preparing the Camera for Initial Use

Charging the Battery

1. Take off the cover on the battery.
2. Put the battery in the charger all the way for you to take it out perfectly. Ensure to do the opposite.
3. Charge the battery.
   - **For LC-E12**
     - Flip out the charger's prongs and plug them into an outlet.
   - **For LC-E12E**

Plug the power cord into the charger and connect it to a power outlet. The recharging process will start automatically, and the charge lamp (1) will turn orange.

When the battery is completely recharged, the full-charge lamp (2) will turn green.

It takes about 2 hours to fully charge a completely depleted battery at room temperature (around 23°C or 73°F). The time needed for charging can vary depending on the temperature and the remaining battery capacity.

Charging in cold temperatures (5-10°C or 41-50°F) will take longer, up to around 4 hours, for safety reasons.

When you first get the battery, it won't be fully charged. You should charge it before using it.

Charge the battery the day before or on the day you plan to use it. Even during storage, a charged battery will slowly lose power and capacity.

After charging the battery, remove it from the charger and unplug the charger from the outlet. If you're not using the camera, take out the battery. Leaving the battery in for a long time can lead to it losing power faster and having a shorter lifespan. Store the battery with the protective cover on. Storing a fully charged battery for a long time may reduce its performance.

The battery charger can also be used in other countries. It's compatible with power sources from 100 VAC to 240 V AC at 50/60 Hz. If needed, use a plug adapter for different countries or regions, but don't connect a voltage transformer to the battery charger as it can damage it.

If the battery runs out quickly even after a full charge, it's likely at the end of its life. You'll need to buy a new battery.

Inserting or Removing Battery

Inserting Battery

1. Ensure to Slide the cover to enable you to open the battery compartment.

2. Put the battery in with the metal part first and push it until it clicks into place.
3. Close the cover by sliding it back until it snaps shut.

Removing Battery

1. Open the cover where the battery goes, and make sure the camera is turned off. Check that a small light is off, then open the cover.
2. Take out the battery.
3. There's a small lever; press it and take out the battery. Always use the provided cover on the battery to avoid electrical problems.

Inserting or Removing Card

Inserting Card

1. Open the cover where you put the memory card.
2. Put the card into the slot with the label facing the back of the camera. Make sure it clicks into place.
3. Close the cover.

Removing Card

1. First, open the cover of the camera after making sure it's turned off. Check if the access lamp is not lit, then open the cover. If the screen shows "Saving...", close the cover.
2. Next, take out the memory card. Push it in gently, and it will pop out. Pull the card straight out and close the cover.

Using the Screen

You can move the screen up and down. Opening wide up to 180 degrees is definitely sure. If you want to see yourself in the camera, turn the screen towards you like a mirror.

Close the screen when you're not using the camera. Also, don't open the screen too hard, or it might break.

Turn on the Power

To start the camera, press the power button. Press it again to stop the camera.

Attaching or Detaching the Lens

Attaching the Lens

1. Take off the caps.
   - Twist and remove the back and body caps as shown in the arrows.
2. Put on the lens.
   - Match the white marks on the lens and camera, then twist the lens until it clicks.
3. Take off the front lens cap.

Detaching the Lens

1. Press the lens release button and turn the lens toward the arrow until it stops. Then, remove the lens.
2. Put the rear lens cap on the removed lens.

Attaching or Detaching EF/EF-S Lenses

Attaching EF/EF-S Lenses

1. Take off the lens caps from the lens, adapter, and camera body.
2. Connect the lens to the adapter. Match the red or white marks on the lens and adapter, then turn the lens until it clicks.
3. Attach the adapter to the camera. Match the white marks on the adapter and camera, then turn the lens until it clicks.
4. Switch the lens's focus mode to <AF> for autofocus. <AF> means autofocus, and <MF> means manual focus, but autofocus won't work in manual mode.

Detaching EF/EF-S Lenses

1. Press the button and twist the adapter following the arrow.
    *   Keep twisting until it stops, then remove it.
2. Take off the lens from the adapter.
    *   Press the release lever and twist the lens to the left.
    *   Twist until it stops, then take it off.
    *   Ensure to place the cap correctly on the back of the lens.

Setting the Screen Display Level

You can choose how things show up on the screen based on what you like. Just do this:

1. Show the main tabs.

   Press the <MENU> button to make the main tabs appear.

2. Pick the Display level tab.

   Use the left or right keys on the cross keys to choose the Display level tab.

Setting the Date/Time/Zone

When you start your device for the first time or if the date, time, or time zone has been reset, follow these steps to set the time zone first.

Setting the time zone first makes it easier to change it later, and your date and time will adjust accordingly.

Make sure to set the date and time because the pictures you take will have this information attached.

1. Choose Date/Time/Zone:

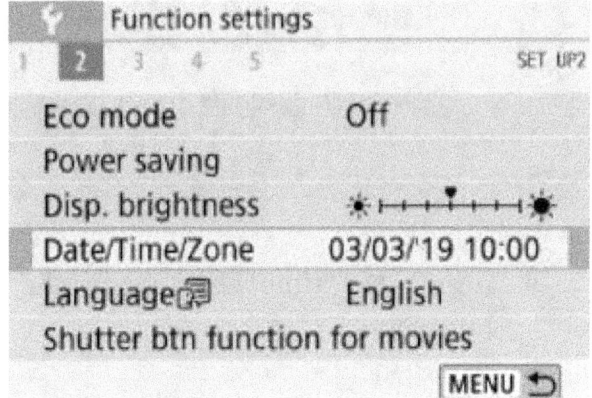

- Use the left or right buttons to pick the option.
- Press [SET].

2. Set Time Zone:
   - Use the left or right buttons to choose the time zone.

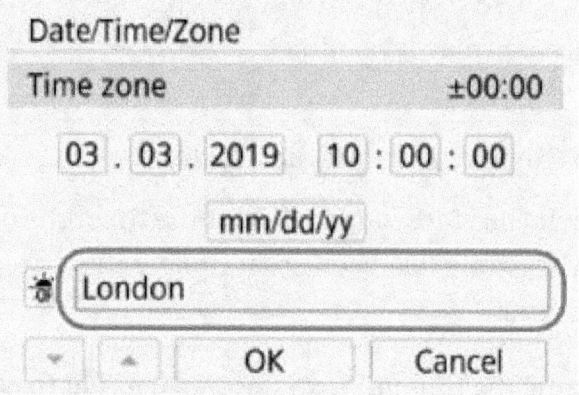

   - Press [SET].

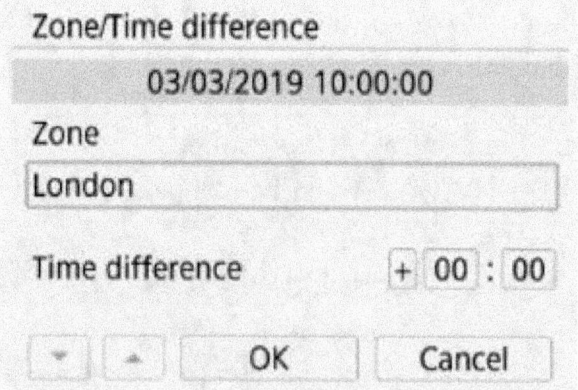

   - Adjust the time zone using the up or down buttons.
   - Press [SET].

- If your time zone isn't listed, press MENU, then set the time difference from UTC.

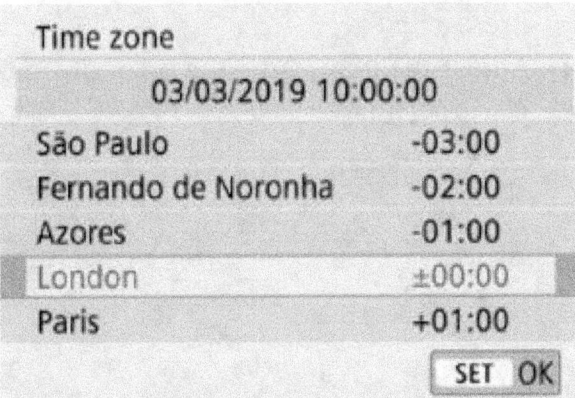

- Use the left or right buttons to select the time difference (+/-/hour/minute).
- Press <SET>.
- Adjust the difference using up or down buttons.
- Press <SET>.
- Once set, choose [OK] using the left or right buttons.
- Press <SET>.

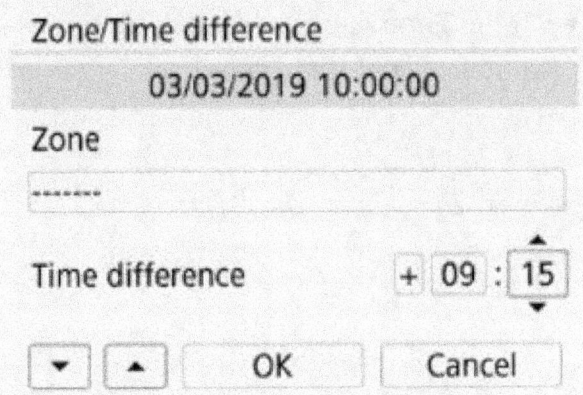

3. Set Date and Time:
   - Use the left or right buttons to select an item.
   - Press <SET>.
   - Adjust the item using the up or down buttons.
   - Press [SET].

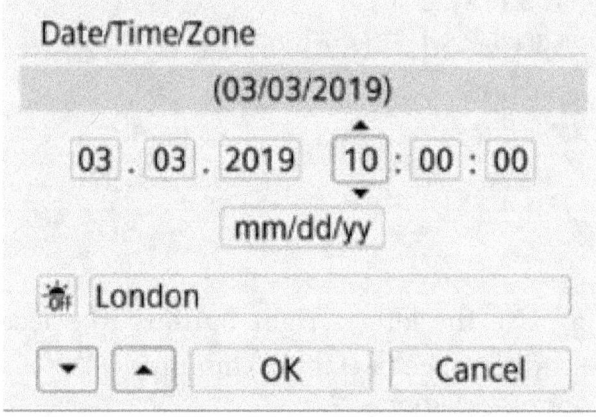

4. Adjust daylight saving time if needed:
   - Press the left or right keys to choose the Time Zone icon, then press <SET>.
   - Use the up or down keys to pick Time Zone, then press <SET>.
   - If the Time Zone is selected, time goes forward by 1 hour. If not, time goes back by 1 hour.

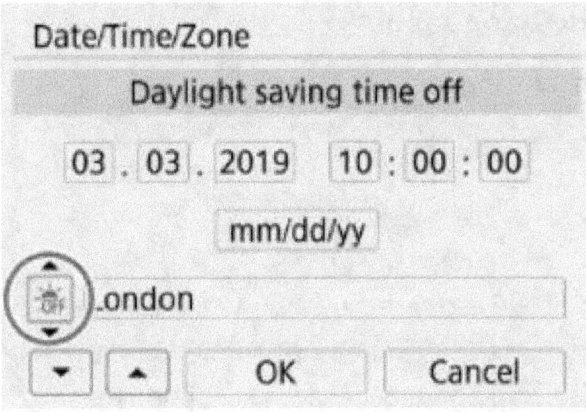

5. To finish, select [OK] using left or right keys.

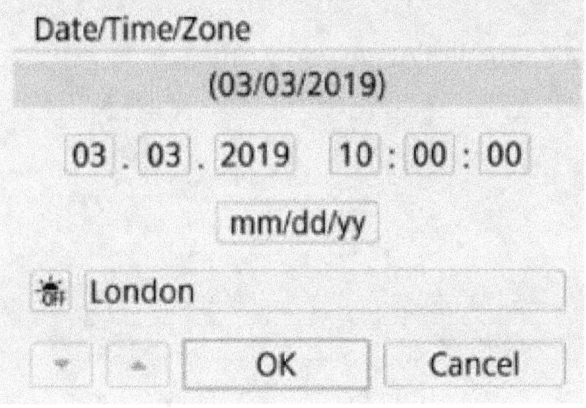

If your camera loses power or gets too cold, the date, time, and time zone settings might reset. If this occurs, you'll need to set them again. Also, check the date, time, and zone after adjusting the time difference setting. These settings need to be correct for the camera to work properly, including temperature control and displaying warnings. And remember, if you're on the date/time/zone screen, the auto power-off time might be longer.

Setting the Language

1. Select [Language].

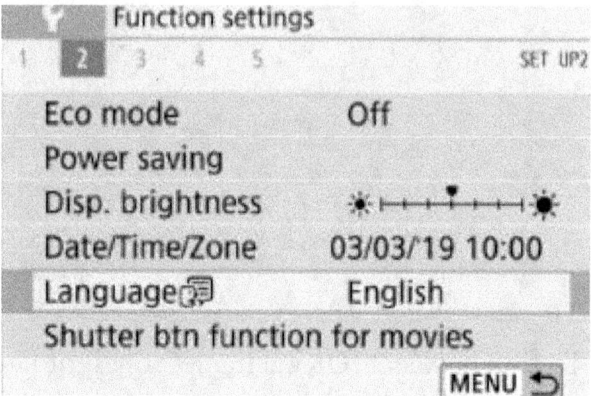

2. Choose the language you want.

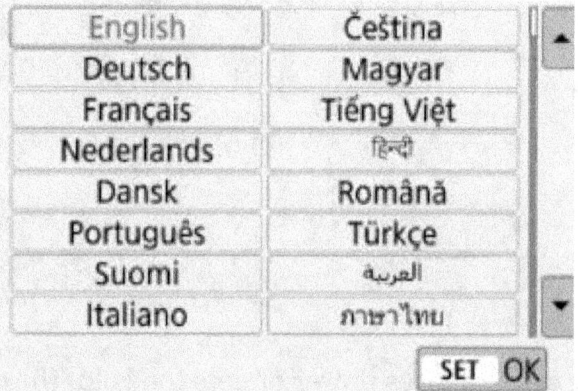

File Numbering

When you take pictures, they're saved in a folder and given numbers from 0001 to 9999. You can change how these numbers work.

1. Go to [File numbering].

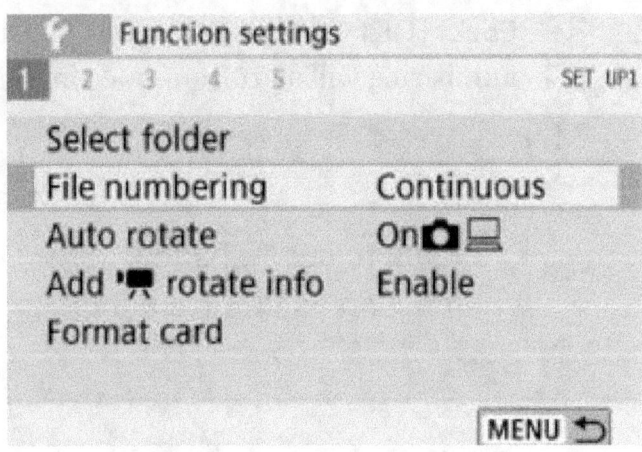

2. Choose [Numbering].

- Select [Continuous] or [Auto reset].

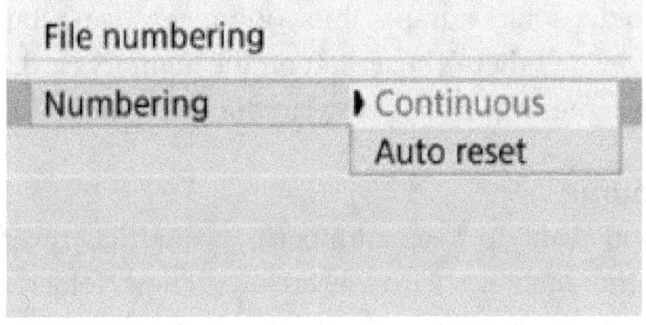

- If you want to start numbering from 0001 again, choose [Manual reset].

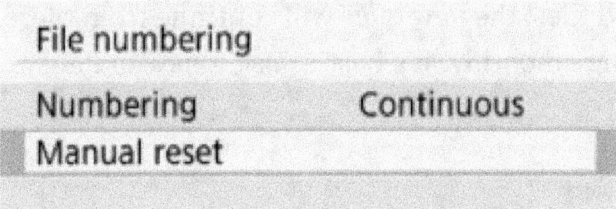

- Click [OK] to make a new folder, and the numbering will start from 0001 in that folder.

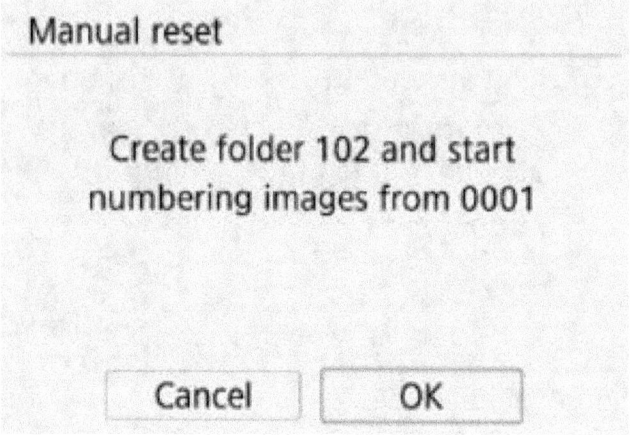

Manual reset

Create folder 102 and start
numbering images from 0001

Cancel   OK

If the folder's file number hits 9999, you can't take more pictures, even if there's space left on the memory card. Instead, you'll see a message saying to swap the card. Put in a new one.

Continuous
When you want to keep numbering your files, even if you change the memory card or create a new folder, the file numbers go on from where they left off. It is helpful when you want to gather pictures from different cards or folders into one place on your computer. If the new card or folder already has numbered files, the new ones will continue from there. To keep numbering smoothly, it's best to use a new memory card each time.

Auto Reset
When you change the memory card or make a new folder, the numbering of saved files starts again from 0001. It helps you

organize images by cards or folders. If the card or folder already has images, the numbering might continue from the existing ones. To start numbering from 0001, use a new card each time.

Manual Reset

If you want to start numbering your files from 0001 again, you can do it manually. When you reset the numbering, a new folder is made, and the files will start from 0001. It is handy to keep your pictures from different days in separate folders.

Menu Operations and Settings

Menu Setting Procedure

With [Menu display] set to [Guided]

1. When you press the <MENU> button, you'll see the main tabs and info about the one you picked.
2. Use the left or right keys to switch between main tabs. You can also turn the mode dial to choose.
3. Press SET to open the menu. Press <M> to go back to the main tab screen.
4. To pick a secondary tab, use the left or right keys or turn the mode dial to choose a Setting.
5. Use the up or down keys to pick a setting, then press SET to pick an Option.
6. Use the up/down or left/right keys to select your desired option. Blue is shown as the current choice.
7. Press SET to confirm your choice. If you change from the default setting, it will turn blue.

8. Press the <MENU> button two times to leave the menu and return to the regular shooting mode.

With [Menu display] set to [Standard]

Ensure to press the MENU button to open the menu screen. Use the left or right keys or turn the mode dial to pick a main or secondary option. Follow the steps from the guided menu setting (starting from step 5) to make your choices. To leave, press the M button.

Dimmed Menu Items

If a menu item looks faded, you can't change it. It's faded because another setting is controlling it. To determine which setting is in control, click the faded menu item and press SET. If you remove the controlling setting, you can change the faded menu item.

Note: Some menu options look faded, and you may not notice the main function replacing them.

Exploring External Camera Features

Topside controls

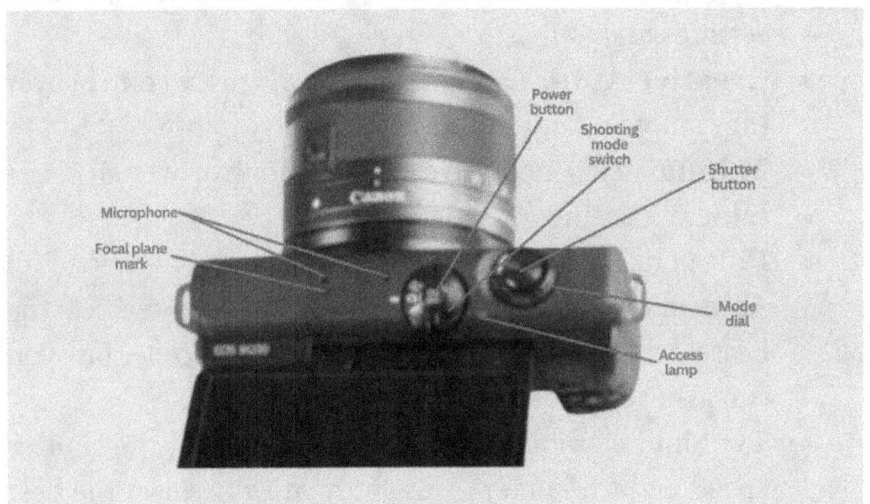

Shutter button: The shutter button is the most important control on the camera, as it is used to take photos. To take a photo, press and hold the shutter button down halfway to focus the camera. Once the camera has focused, a green focus indicator light will appear in the viewfinder. You can then press the shutter button down all the way to take the photo.

Mode Dial: The mode dial allows you to select different shooting modes. Each shooting mode has its own settings, which can be used to control different aspects of the camera, such as the aperture, shutter speed, and ISO speed.

The following are some of the most common shooting modes:

- **Full Auto:** The camera automatically selects the best settings for the scene.
- **Scene Intelligent Auto:** The camera selects the best settings for the scene, but you can also adjust some settings manually.
- **Creative Auto:** This mode gives you more control over the camera's settings, but it's still easy to use.
- **Manual:** This mode gives you full control over all of the camera's settings.
- **P:** Program mode is a good middle ground between Full Auto and Manual. The camera automatically selects the best aperture and shutter speed for the scene, but you can also adjust other settings manually.
- **Tv:** Shutter priority mode allows you to set the shutter speed and the camera will automatically select the best aperture for the scene.
- **Av:** Aperture priority mode allows you to set the aperture and the camera will automatically select the best shutter speed for the scene.
- **M:** Manual mode gives you full control over all of the camera's settings.

Power button: The power button is used to turn the camera on and off. To turn the camera on, press and hold the power button for about 1 second. To turn the camera off, press and hold the power button for about 2 seconds.

Shooting mode switch: The shooting mode switch allows you to select between still photo and video recording modes. To switch to video recording mode, slide the switch to the video position. To switch back to still photo mode, slide the switch to the photo position.

Flash: The flash is used to provide additional light when taking photos or recording videos in low-light conditions. To raise the flash, press the flash release button. To lower the flash, press the flash release button again.

Focal plane mark: The focal plane mark is a line on the top of the camera that indicates the plane of focus. The plane of focus is the imaginary plane that runs parallel to the camera sensor and passes through the point where the light rays converge. When the subject is in focus, the image will be sharpest at the focal plane mark.

Microphone: The microphone is used to record sound when taking movies. To record sound with the microphone, turn the microphone switch on.

Access lamp: The access lamp indicates that the camera is accessing the memory card. When the access lamp is lit, do not remove the memory card.

Front features

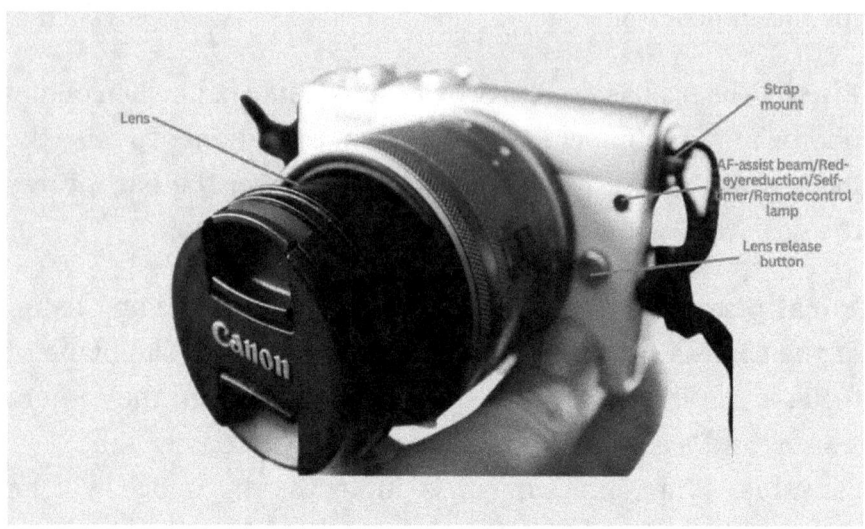

EF-M lens mount index: The EF-M lens mount index is a small white dot on the front of the camera that aligns with the white dot on the lens. This ensures that the lens is properly mounted on the camera.

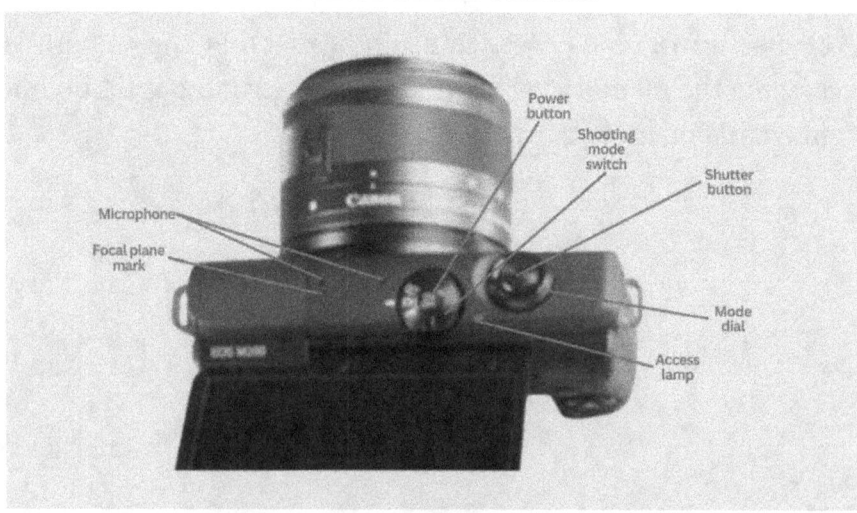

Image sensor: The image sensor is the heart of the camera. It is responsible for capturing the light from the scene and converting it into an digital image. The EOS M200 has a 24.1 megapixel APS-C sized image sensor.

Contacts: The contacts on the front of the camera are used to connect to the lens. They transmit power and data between the camera and the lens.

Strap mount: The strap mount is used to attach a neck strap to the camera. This allows you to carry the camera around your neck for easy access.

Flash up lever: The flash up lever is used to raise the flash. To raise the flash, press the flash up lever. To lower the flash, press the flash release button.

Terminal cover: The terminal cover protects the HDMI OUT terminal and Digital terminal from dust and moisture.

AF-assist beam/Red-eye reduction/Self-timer/Remote control lamp: The AF-assist beam is used to help the camera focus in low-light conditions. The red-eye reduction lamp helps to reduce red-eye in flash photos. The self-timer lamp flashes when the self-timer is counting down. The remote control lamp flashes when the camera is being controlled remotely.

Card slot cover: The card slot cover protects the memory card slot from dust and moisture.

Lens release button: The lens release button is used to release the lens from the camera. To release the lens, press and hold the lens release button while rotating the lens counterclockwise.

Lens lock pin: The lens lock pin prevents the lens from accidentally being released from the camera. To lock the lens, press the lens lock pin into the locked position. To unlock the lens, press the lens lock pin into the unlocked position.

Lens mount: The lens mount is where the lens is attached to the camera. The EOS M200 has an EF-M lens mount.

HDMI OUT terminal: The HDMI OUT terminal is used to connect the camera to an HDTV or other external display device.

Digital terminal: The Digital terminal is used to connect the camera to a computer or other digital device.

Speaker: The speaker is used to play back audio from recorded videos.

Back-of-the-body controls

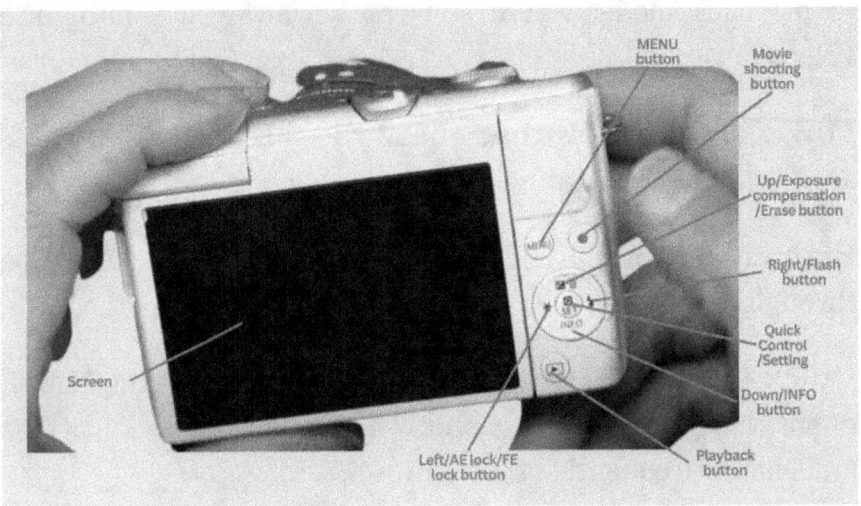

Screen: The 3-inch vari-angle touchscreen is the main interface for controlling the camera and reviewing photos and videos. It can be tilted 180 degrees for selfies and other creative angles.

Menu button: The Menu button opens the camera's menu system, where you can change all of the camera's settings.

Up/Exposure compensation/Erase button: The Up button is used to navigate through menus and select items. It is also used to increase the exposure compensation. To erase a photo or video, press and hold the Up button.

Down/Info button: The Down button is used to navigate through menus and select items. It is also used to display the shooting information on the screen.

Playback button: The Playback button switches the camera to playback mode, where you can review your photos and videos.

Movie shooting button: The Movie shooting button starts and stops video recording.

Right/Flash button: The Right button is used to navigate through menus and select items. It is also used to fire the flash.

Quick Control/Setting: The Quick Control/Setting button opens the Quick Control menu, where you can quickly access and change frequently used settings.

Left/AE lock/FE lock button: The Left button is used to navigate through menus and select items. It is also used to lock the auto exposure (AE) or flash exposure (FE).

AE lock/FE lock button: When the AE lock button is pressed, the camera will lock the exposure at the current setting. This can be useful when shooting in scenes with mixed lighting. When the FE lock button is pressed, the camera will lock the flash exposure at the current setting. This can be useful when shooting with a flash in different lighting conditions.

Working with Memory Cards

1. The number of pictures you can take depends on your memory card's space, camera settings, and more.

2. Don't mess with the card or battery when the camera's light is on—it means data is being saved or transferred, and you could ruin your photos or camera.

3. Also, don't remove the card or battery, shake or hit the camera, or unplug the power cord when the light is on.

4. If there are existing pictures on the card, the new ones might not start from 0001; they might start from a different number, like 430.

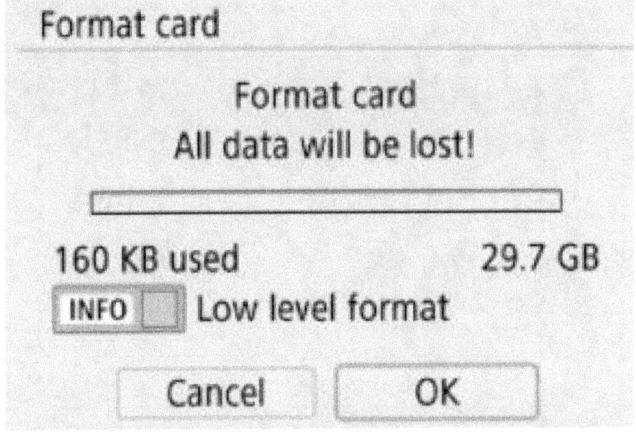

If your device shows a card error, take out the card and put it back. If the error continues, try using a different card. If you can transfer photos to a computer, do that and then format the card in your camera. Avoid touching the card's metal parts, and keep them clean. Also, use something other than Multimedia cards (MMC), as they won't work.

CHAPTER 2: CONTROLLING FOCUS AND DEPTH OF FIELD

AF Operation

1. Choose how the camera focuses.

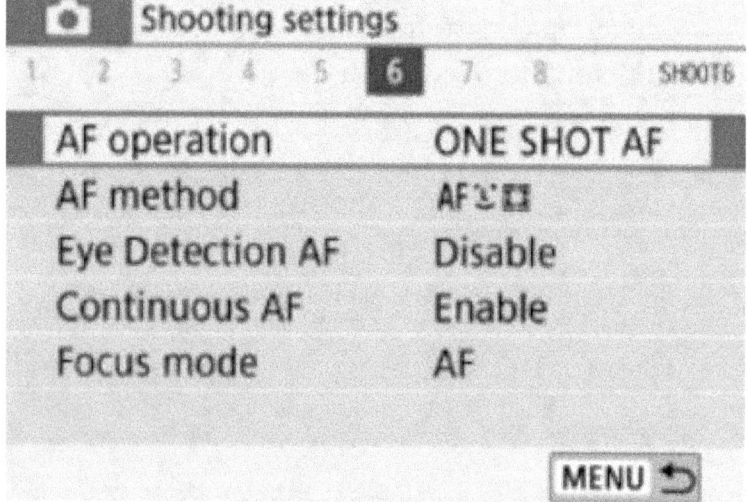

2. Pick a specific setting for focusing.

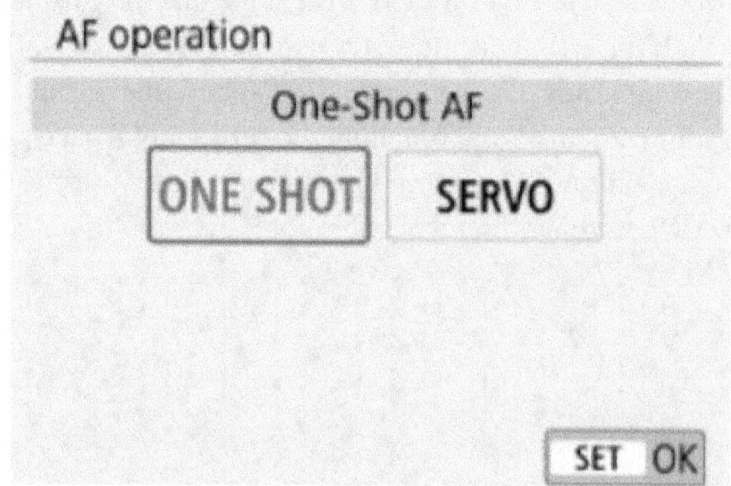

If the camera can't focus, a light will turn orange. If this happens, you can't take a picture, even if you press the button. Adjust your shot and try focusing again, or check the guide for tricky shooting conditions.

One-Shot AF for Still Subjects (ONE SHOT)

This focusing mode is best for things that aren't moving. Just press the shutter button halfway, and the camera will focus just once.

When the focus is right, the AF point turns green, and it beeps. The focus stays locked as long as you keep the shutter button halfway pressed, so you can change the framing of the shot before taking the picture.

If you turn off the "Beep" option in settings, the device won't make a sound when it focuses.

Servo AF for Moving Subjects (SERVO)

This way of focusing is great for things that are moving. Just press the shutter button halfway and the camera will keep adjusting the focus as long as you hold it that way.

When it gets the focus right, the AF point will turn blue, and that's when the photo will be taken with the correct exposure.

Uses auto selection AF in Zone AF frames to cover a large area, which makes focusing easier than with 1-point AF. Prioritizes focusing on the nearest subject. Faces of any people in the

ZoneAF frame are also given priority in focusing.AF points in focus are displayed with [1-point AF].

AF Method

You can choose how the camera focuses based on the situation or who you're taking a picture of. It focuses on people's faces within a specific area you pick.

Face+Tracking

The camera can find and focus on people's faces. It puts an AF point over the detected face and keeps it in focus.

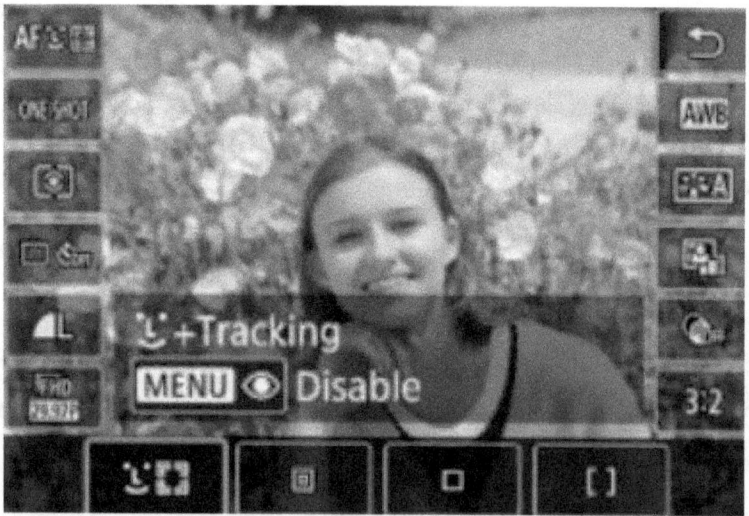

If no face is found, the camera uses the entire AF area to autofocus automatically.

With Servo AF, it keeps focusing on moving subjects within the Area AF frame while you take photos.

Spot AF

The camera focuses on a smaller area with 1-point AF.

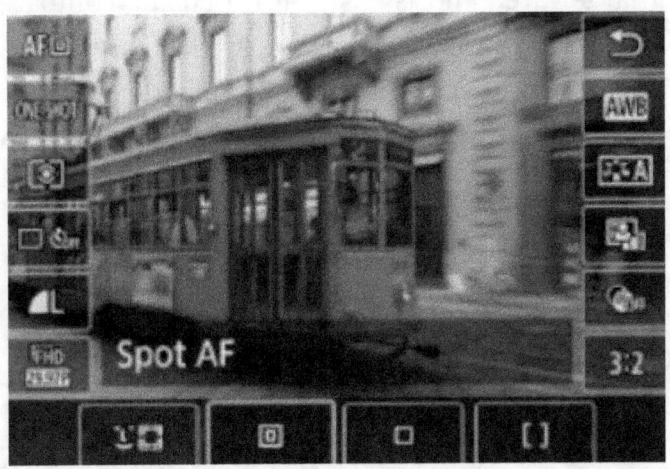

1-point AF

The camera focuses by using just one focus point.

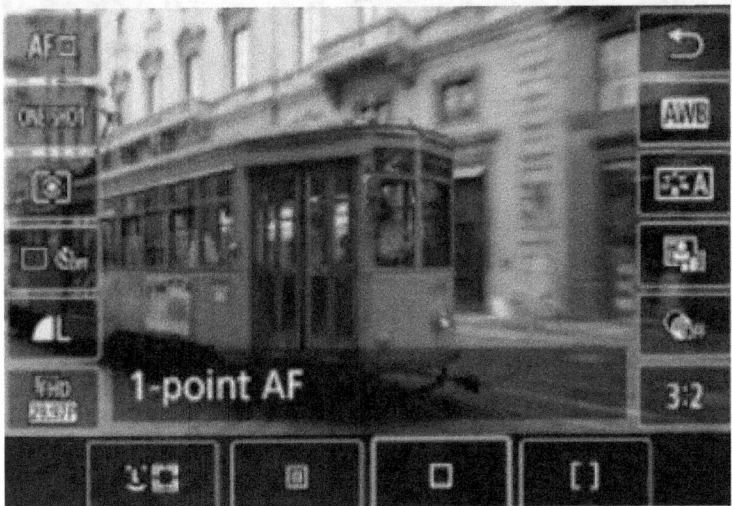

Zone AF

It uses auto selection AF within the Zone AF frames, which covers a larger area and is easier for focusing compared to 1-point AF. It gives priority to focusing on the closest subject and also prioritizes focusing on the faces of people in the Zone AF frame. The AF points in focus are shown with [1-point AF].

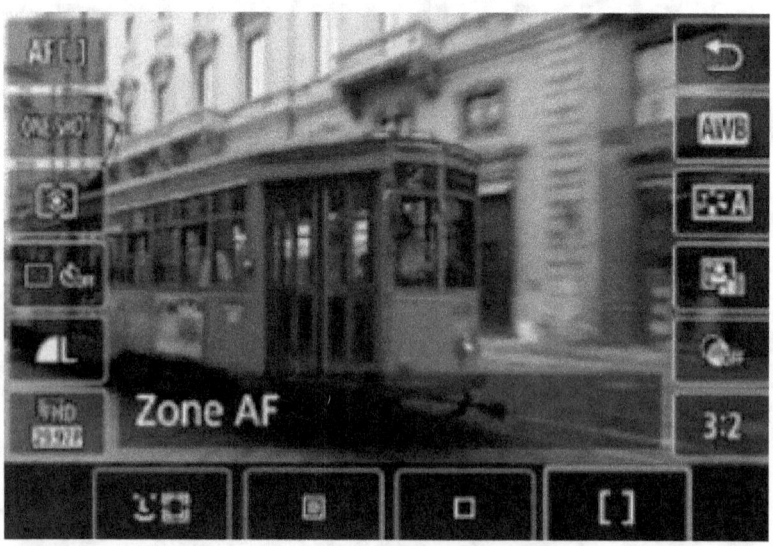

Selecting the AF Method

You can decide how the camera focuses depending on what you're taking a picture of or the environment you're in.

If you want to focus manually:

1. Pick [AF method].

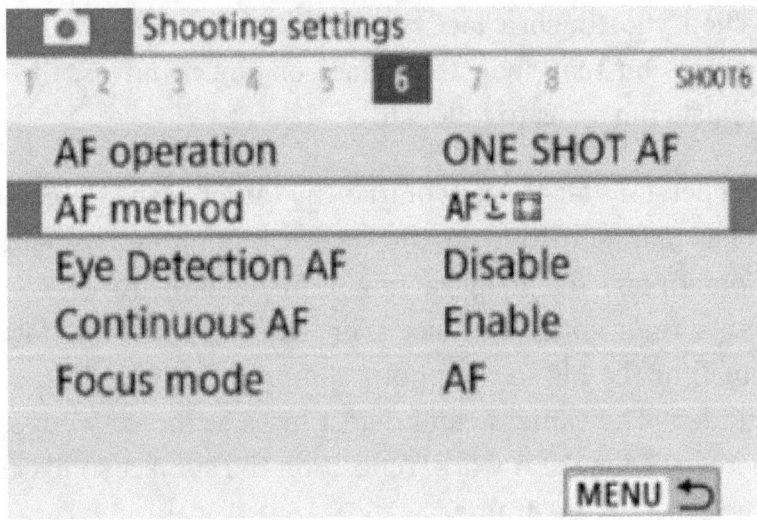

2. Choose a setting.

(face)+Tracking

The camera can find and focus on people's faces. If a face moves, the focus point also moves to follow it.

1. Look for the AF point. It appears over any detected face.
2. Focus on your subject
   When you press the shutter button halfway, the AF point turns green, and you'll hear a beep when the subject is in focus. If the AF point is orange, it means the camera couldn't focus on the subject.

3. Take your picture.

Tapping a Face for Focus

When you touch a face or object on the screen, the camera focuses on that spot. If the face or object moves, the camera adjusts the focus to follow it.

If a person's face is very blurry, the camera can't detect it. First, focus manually to make the face clear, and then use autofocus. Sometimes, the camera might mistakenly think something other than a face is a face. This can happen if the face is too small or too big in the photo, too bright or too dark, or partly hidden. The camera can't detect faces at the very edges of the screen. To make it work, reposition the subject so it's closer to the center of the frame.

Spot AF/1-point AF/Zone AF

You can choose where the camera focuses manually, and we'll use 1-point AF screens as an example.

1. Choose where you want to focus by tapping on the screen. If you're using Zone AF, a frame will appear around the chosen zone.
2. Move the focus point by tapping the screen where you want to focus. To center it again, tap the Zoom icon. You can also zoom in by tapping the Zoom icon multiple times.
3. Once the focus point is where you want it, press the shutter button halfway. If it turns green and you hear a beep, the camera is focused. If it turns orange, it means the focus is not right.
4. After achieving focus, take the picture by fully pressing the shutter button.

Note:

- When using Servo AF, the camera tries to follow and focus on moving subjects by moving the active AF point.
- However, in certain situations, like when the subjects are very small, it might not work well.
- If you have trouble getting focus assistance from an AF point at the screen's edge, try using an AF point in the center.

AF Shooting Tips

- Sometimes, even if you've already focused, pressing the shutter button halfway will focus again. This might also cause changes in image brightness.
- Depending on what you're shooting and the conditions, it might take longer to focus, or the camera's ability to take continuous shots quickly may decrease.
- If the lighting changes while you're taking pictures, the screen might flicker, and focusing can be tricky. In such cases, restart the camera and continue taking pictures with autofocus under the lighting you intend to use.
- If the autofocus can't focus correctly, try manually focusing instead.
- If the subject at the edge of the frame isn't quite in focus, you can center it using the autofocus point or frame, get it in focus, and then recompose your shot before taking the picture.

- Some lenses might take a bit more time to focus automatically, and they might not always focus precisely.

Shooting Conditions that Make Focusing Difficult

- When the subject lacks contrast, like a plain blue sky or solid-colored surfaces, or if there are extremely bright or dark areas.
- In low-light conditions.
- When the subject has patterns that only contrast horizontally.
- With subjects that have repetitive patterns (e.g., skyscraper windows or computer keyboards).
- When dealing with very fine lines or faint subject outlines.
- Under changing or flickering light sources.
- In night scenes or with small points of light.
- When there's flickering under fluorescent or LED lights.
- With extremely tiny subjects.
- If the subject is near the edge of the screen.
- For subjects that are highly reflective or backlit (e.g., shiny cars).
- When your autofocus point covers both near and distant subjects.
- When the subject keeps moving and doesn't stay still, possibly due to camera shake or subject motion.
- If the subject is very out of focus.
- When a soft focus effect is used, like with a special lens or filter.

- If there's noise or unusual visual artifacts during autofocus..

Eye Detection AF

When you use the AF method called "[u+Tracking]," the camera is able to focus on people's eyes.

Here's how to use Eye Detection AF:

1. Choose "Eye Detection AF" from your camera settings.

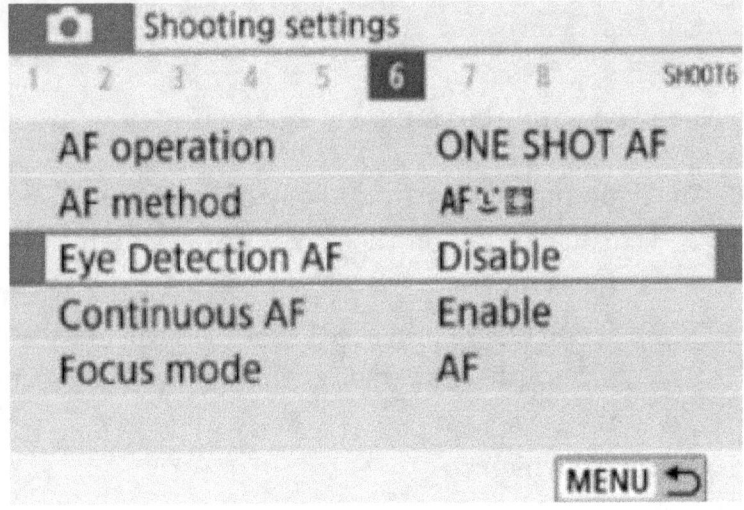

2. Turn it "On" to enable this feature.

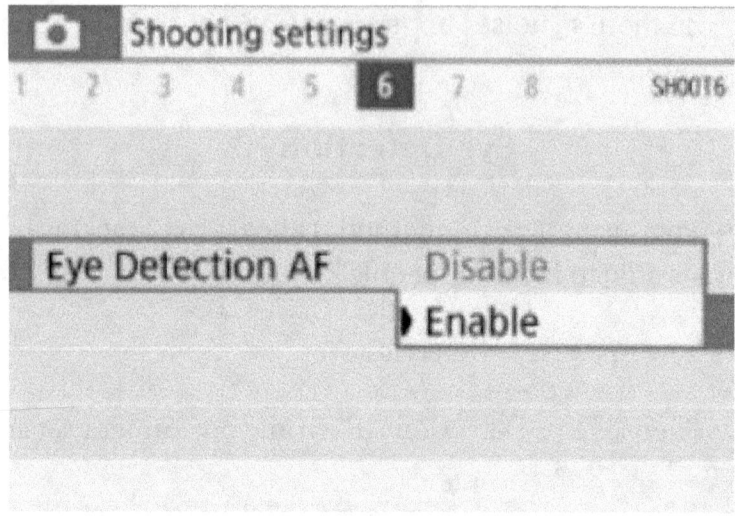

Now, when you point the camera at a person:

1. An AF point appears around one of their eyes.
    - You can tap on the screen to select which eye to focus on.
    - If you tap on other parts of their face, like the nose or mouth, the camera will automatically focus on the eyes.
2. Capture the picture.

Note:

Sometimes, the camera might not accurately find the subject's eyes, depending on the person and the lighting.

You can turn on "Eye Detection AF" by going to the Quick Control screen and selecting it. This option is available when you've already chosen "[Face+Tracking]" as your AF method. To get there, press the <MENU> button and then press SET.

Continuous AF

1. Choose "Continuous AF" in the camera settings.

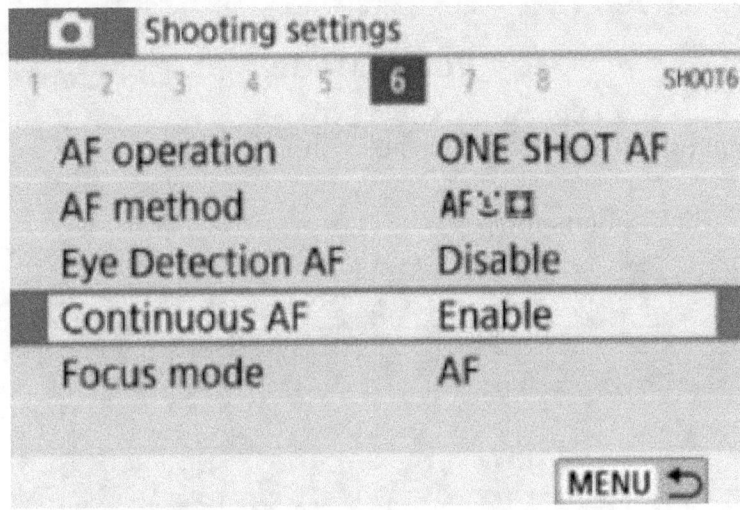

2. Turn on the option called "Enable."

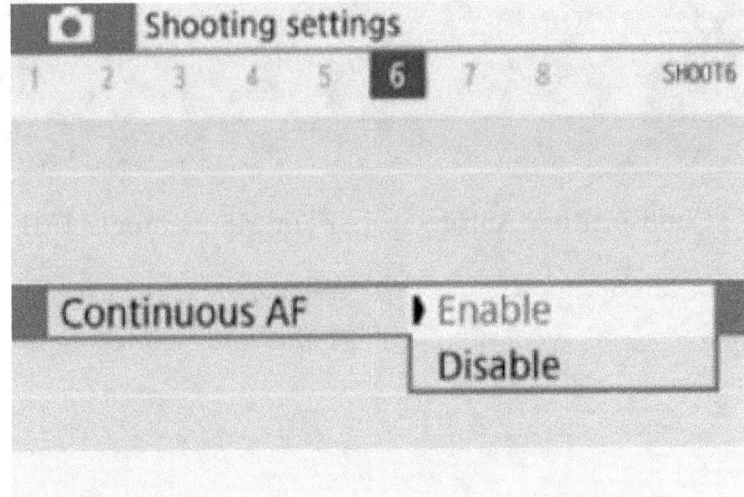

Turning on this feature uses up the battery faster and limits the number of photos you can take, as the lens keeps moving continuously.

Focus Mode

Choose how the camera focuses with EF-M lenses:

1. Pick "Focus mode."

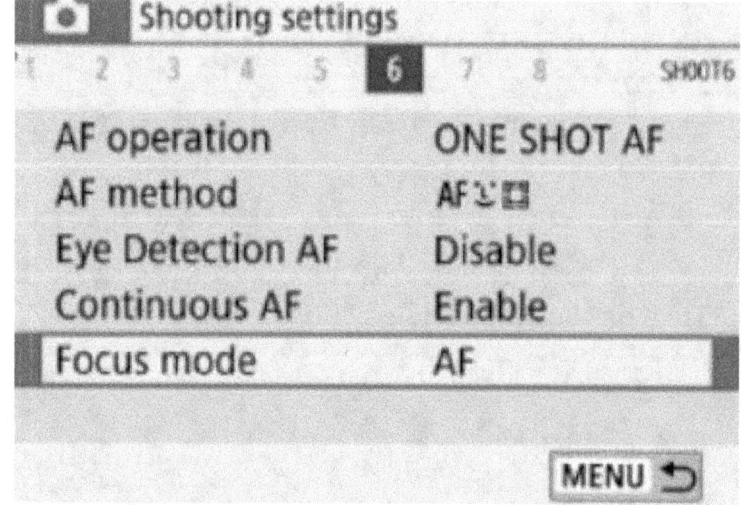

2. Choose either Autofocus [AF] or Manual focus [MF].

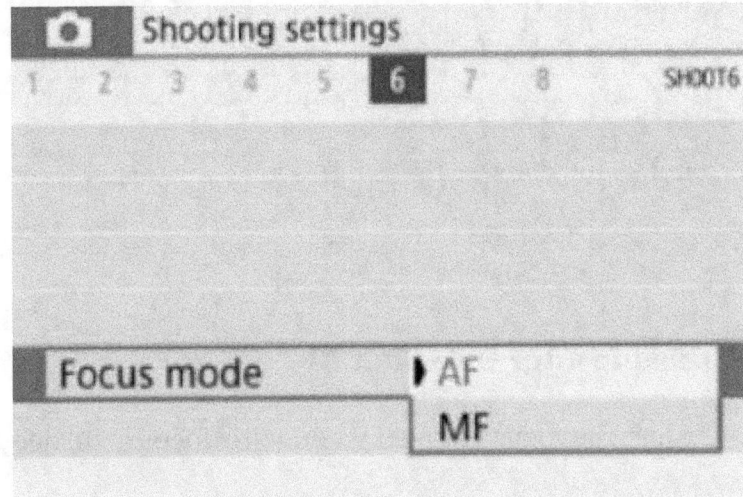

Manually Focusing with a Lens after AF

1. Choose the manual focus option for your camera lenses.

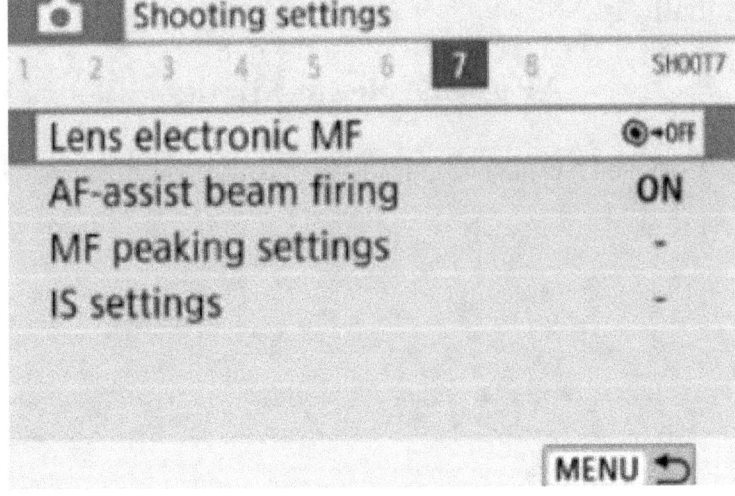

2. Pick a setting for how you want to adjust the focus.

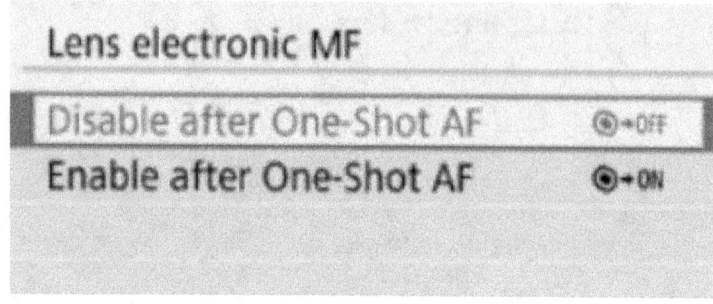

Disable after One-Shot AF

Adjust the focus yourself when auto-focus is turned off.

Enable after One-Shot AF

You can change the focus yourself after the camera focuses automatically by holding the shutter button halfway.

AF-Assist Beam Firing

1. Choose [AF-assist beam firing] on the camera.

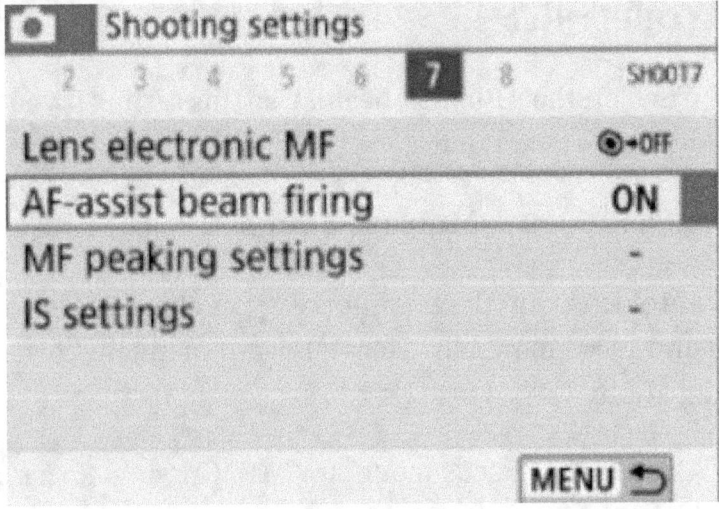

2. Pick an option from the menu.

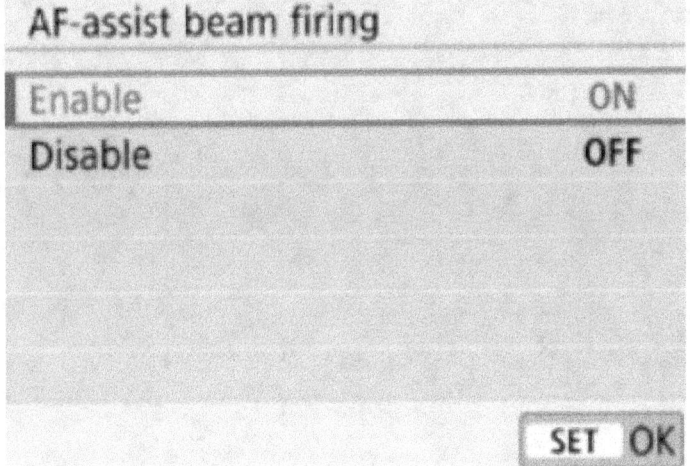

[ON] Enable

Allows the camera to use a helpful light to focus better in low light conditions.

[OFF] Disable

Turn off the AF-assist beam. Use this setting if you don't want the beam to fire.

Manual Focus

If the autofocus can't focus properly, you can zoom in on the image and focus manually. Here's how to manually focus with magnification:

1. Change the "Focus mode" to "MF" (Manual Focus). Turn the lens's focus ring to get a rough focus.

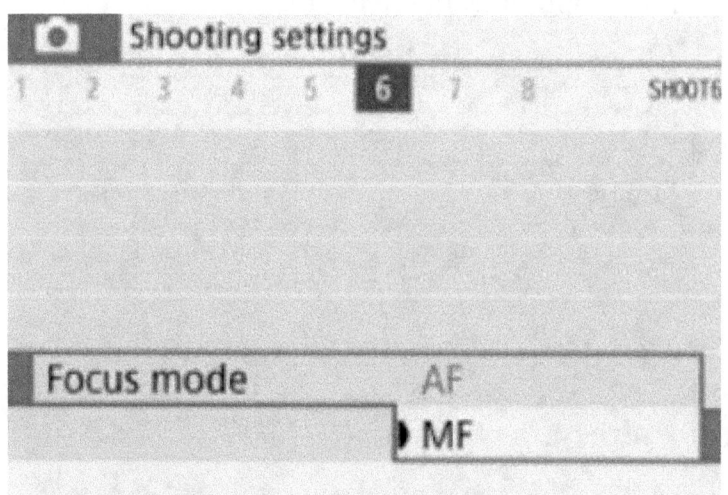

2. Zoom in on the image:
   Each time you tap the Zoom icon, the screen gets closer.

3. Pick the area you want to zoom in on:

After tapping, you can slide your finger to move the magnified view.

4. Focus manually:
   While you're looking at the magnified view, turn the lens's focus ring to get the focus right.

   When you're done focusing, tap the Zoom icon again to go back to the regular view.

5. Take your picture.

If you're using lenses other than EF-M ones, make sure to switch the lens to "MF" (Manual Focus) first. Even when you're in manual focus, you can still use the Touch Shutter feature to take pictures effortlessly.

Setting MF Peaking

When you focus manually, the camera can highlight the edges of things that are in focus with color, which helps you focus better. You can pick the color and change how sensitive this highlighting is.

Here's how to use manual focus peaking:

1. Go to "MF peaking setting" in your camera settings.

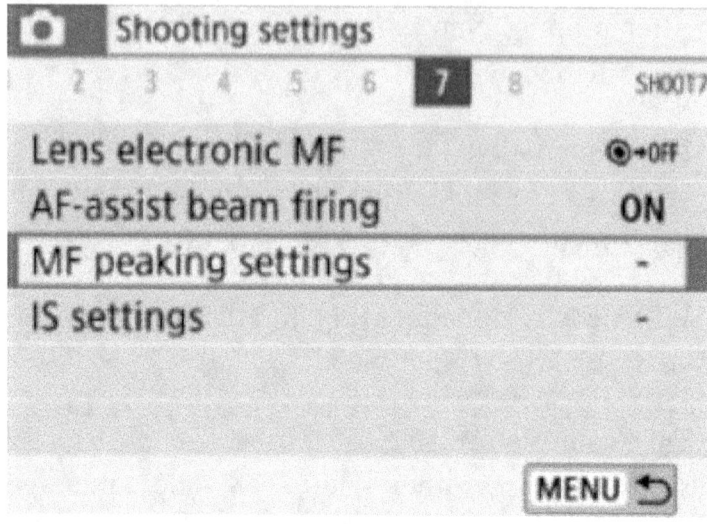

2. Turn on "Peaking" by selecting "On."

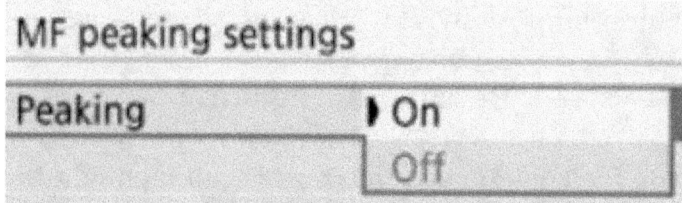

3. Adjust the level and choose the color according to your needs.

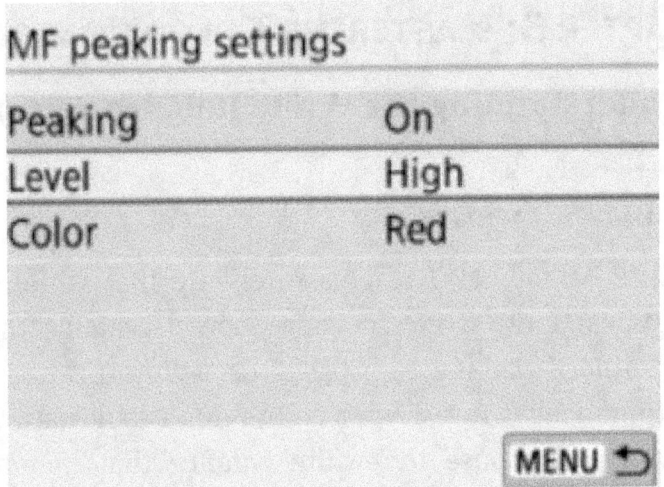

Note:

- The peaking highlight won't appear when you zoom in on the image.
- Sometimes, it might be difficult to see peaking details if you're using a high ISO setting, especially with expanded ISO options. You can make it easier to see by lowering the ISO or turning off the peaking if needed.
- Keep in mind that the peaking highlights you see on the screen won't show up in the actual photos you take.

CHAPTER 3: MASTERING COLOR CONTROLS

Understanding the White Balance Setting

White Balance setting

White balance (WB) helps to ensure that white objects appear truly white in your photos. Usually, the Auto setting, either "Ambience priority" or "White priority," does this automatically. But if your colors don't look natural with Auto, you can choose the white balance that matches the lighting or set it yourself by photographing something white.

Here's how to adjust the white balance:

1. Go to ": White balance" in your settings.
2. Pick one of the options available.

When we look at something white, it appears white no matter the light source. But in digital cameras, they pick a color reference based on the type of light (like daylight or indoor light) and then use software to make white things look genuinely white in the pictures. This way, your photos have natural colors.

[AWB] Auto white balance setting

Choose "White balance" from your camera settings. Then, pick "AWB" to make warm colors in your photos look stronger in tungsten lighting. If you choose "AWB w," it will reduce the strong, warm colors in your pictures.

To do this, follow these steps:

1. Go to "White balance."
2. Pick "AWB."
3. Press the INFO button and select the desired option.

Cautions for Setting [AWB w]

The warm colors in your pictures might become less noticeable.

If there are different types of lights in the scene, the warm color might not go away.

When you use a flash, the colors will be similar to using the "Auto White Balance" setting.

Custom White Balance setting

You can use custom white balance to set the correct white balance for the specific lighting where you're taking your photos. Remember to do this where you're actually shooting, under the same lighting conditions.

Here's how to set a custom white balance:

1. Take a picture of something completely white. Use manual focus and take the shot with the standard exposure settings.
2. Go to ": Custom White Balance" in your camera settings.
3. Choose the picture you took earlier, then press "SET" and select "OK" to use its data.
4. Now, go to ": White Balance."

5. Pick the custom white balance you just created.

Note:

- If the brightness when you take the first picture is very different from the normal setting, you might not get the right white balance.
- You can't use images that were taken in "Monochrome" mode, had creative filters added before or after shooting, were cropped, or were taken with a different camera.
- If there are images you can't use, your camera might show them.
- Instead of photographing a white object, you can also use a gray chart or a standard 18% gray reflector that you can buy.

Color Temperature

1. Choose the "White Balance" option.
2. Pick "K" for color temperature.
3. Use the dial to set the color temperature between 2500K and 10000K, then press SET.

Note:

- When you're adjusting the color temperature for artificial lighting, you might need to tweak the white balance correction by adding a bit of magenta or green.
- If you set the color temperature to what you read with a special tool called a color temperature meter, take some test photos. Adjust the setting to make up for any

difference between the meter's reading and what the camera thinks the color temperature should be.

White Balance Correction

Correcting the white balance has a similar effect to using a color filter that you can buy to adjust color temperature. Here's how you do it:

1. Go to ": WB correction" in your camera settings.
2. Use the arrow keys to move the "+" symbol to where you want it.
   - B is for making the image more blue.
   - A is for making it more amber.
   - M is for making it more magenta.
   - G is for making it more green.
   - The color balance of the image will shift in the direction you choose. On the right of the screen, "Shift" shows the direction and how much correction you've made.
   - If you want to remove all white balance corrections, select "Clear all."
   - Press "SET" to save your changes and exit the setting.

Note:

Changing the white balance is like adjusting the colors in your camera. You can do this by selecting WB correction and moving the marker to change the colors (B for blue, A for amber, M for magenta, G for green). The image's colors will shift based on your choice. To clear the settings or exit, press SET.

Taking a Quick Look at Picture Styles

You can quickly adjust how your photos look by picking a Picture Style preset:

1. Go to ": Picture Style" in your settings.
2. Choose the Picture Style you want from the options.

Picture Style Characteristics

[A] Auto

The camera will automatically adjust the color to fit the scene. This makes colors look vibrant, especially for things like blue skies, green landscapes, and sunsets, particularly in outdoor and nature scenes.

If the automatic setting doesn't give you the color you want, you can try using a different Picture Style.

[S] Standard

The picture appears bright, clear, and sharp. This is a versatile Picture Style that works well for most situations.

[P] Portrait

This mode is designed to make skin look good. It gives the image a softer look and is great for close-up portraits. You can also tweak the skin tone by adjusting the "Color tone" setting.

Landscape

This mode makes blues and greens really stand out, and your pictures will be super clear and sharp. It's great for creating stunning landscape shots.

Fine Detail

This mode is good for capturing fine details and textures in your subject. The colors will be a bit more vibrant.

Neutral

Use this mode if you plan to edit the image on a computer. It creates pictures with natural colors and a more subtle, less intense look in terms of brightness and color richness.

Faithful

This mode is meant for editing images on a computer. It adjusts the colors of a subject captured in sunlight (5200K) to match the actual colors of the subject. The result is photos with more subdued and natural-looking colors, not too bright or overly vibrant.

Monochrome

This mode makes pictures without colors, just in black and white.

Picture Style Customization

1. Choose a Picture Style.
2. Pick the specific style you want.
3. Adjust the settings by selecting an item and setting its value. You can find details about these settings on page 160 under "Settings and Effects."
4. Save your changes by pressing the SET button. Your adjusted settings will appear in blue.

CHAPTER 4: CHOOSING BASIC PICTURE SETTINGS

Basic Shooting Mode

Scene Intelligent Auto/Hybrid Auto (Fully Automatic)

Scene Intelligent Auto/Hybrid Auto (Fully Automatic) is a smart mode in your camera. It figures out the best settings for your photos or videos without you having to do anything. It can focus on still or moving objects by detecting their movement.

With this mode, you can create a short video by taking pictures. The camera records short clips before each photo and later combines them into a video.

To use this mode:

1. Turn the shooting mode switch to A+. To use a specific mode, like <M>, after switching the mode, tap the upper left of the screen, use the < or > keys to choose the mode, and press SET.

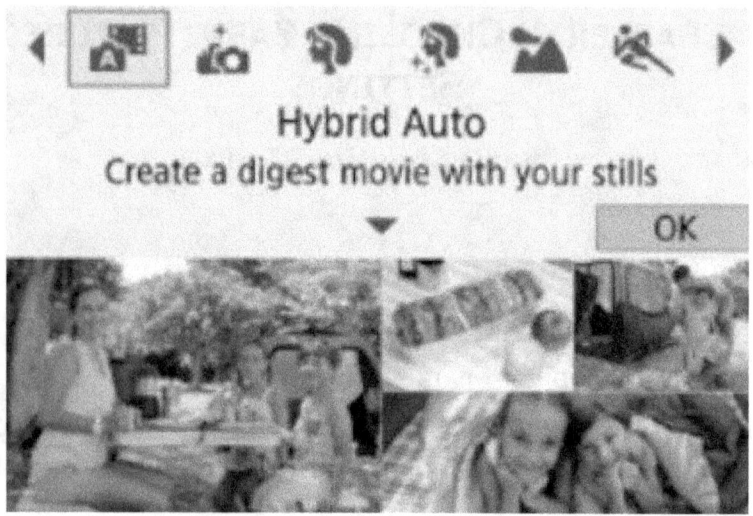

2. Point the camera at what you want to photograph (the subject). Sometimes, a frame might appear around the subject, depending on the shooting conditions. If there are people in the shot, you may see AF points over their faces.

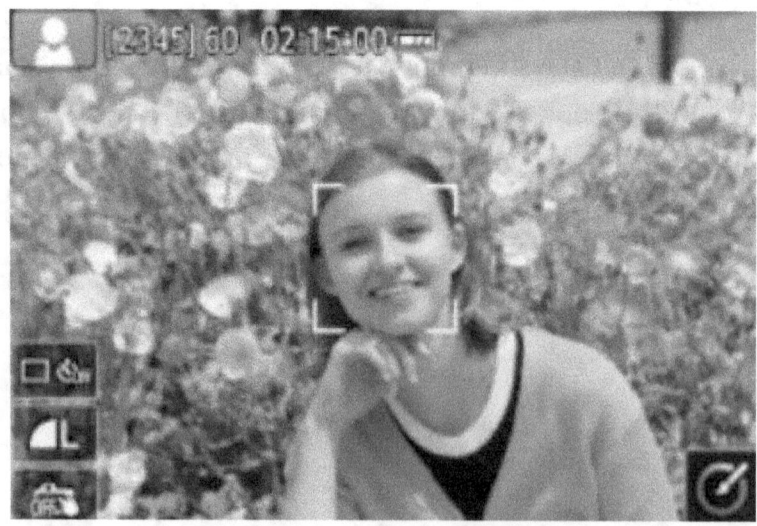

3. Focus on your subject:
   - Gently press the shutter button halfway to make sure the camera focuses.
   - If a symbol blinks, use a lever to raise the flash if you need it.
   - You can also tap on a person's face or any object on the screen to focus (Touch AF).
   - In low light, a helpful light might turn on automatically to assist with focusing.
   - If your subject isn't moving, a green point will show when it's in focus, and the camera beeps (One-Shot AF).
   - If your subject moves, a blue point shows and follows the movement (Servo AF).
4. Take the picture:
   - Press the shutter button down to capture the picture.
   - The picture you took will be shown on the screen for about 2 seconds.
   - To close the flash, gently push it down using your fingers.

Minimizing Blurred Photos

Use a strong tripod for your camera that can handle its weight. Make sure to attach the camera tightly to the tripod. It's a good idea to use a wireless remote control, which you need to buy separately.

Recomposing the Shot

Depending on the scene, placing your subject to the left or right can give your photo a more balanced background and better perspective.

When you have a stationary subject, you can focus on it by pressing the shutter button halfway. The focus will lock onto that subject. While keeping the shutter button halfway pressed, you can recompose your shot, and then press the shutter button fully to capture the image. This technique is known as "focus lock."

Shooting a Moving Subject (mode only)

Once you press the shutter button halfway and see a blue AF point, the camera will track moving subjects and continuously adjust the focus using Servo AF. Make sure to keep the subject within the frame while holding the shutter button halfway. When you're ready to capture the perfect moment, press the shutter button all the way down.

Scene Icons

The camera figures out what's happening and adjusts its settings accordingly. It shows the detected scene type on the top left of the screen.

Special Scene Modes

Here are some special camera modes:

1. **Self Portrait Mode:** For taking pictures of yourself.

2. **Portrait Mode:** Captures clear photos of people.

3. **Smooth Skin Mode:** Makes skin look smoother in photos.

4. **Landscape Mode:** Ideal for capturing wide outdoor scenes.

5. **Sports Mode:** Great for capturing fast-moving action, like sports events.

6. **Close-up Mode:** Perfect for detailed shots of small objects.

7. **Food Mode:** Optimized for taking delicious food photos.

8. **Night Portrait Mode:** Helps capture people in low-light settings.

9. **Handheld Night Scene Mode:** Takes clear photos at night, even without a tripod.

10. **HDR Backlight Control Mode:** Ensures balanced photos in challenging lighting.

11. **Silent Mode:** Takes photos quietly without any noise.

Self Portrait Mode

To take pictures of yourself, use Self Portrait mode. Just turn the screen towards you. You can customize the pictures by smoothing your skin, adjusting brightness, and changing the background to make yourself look better.

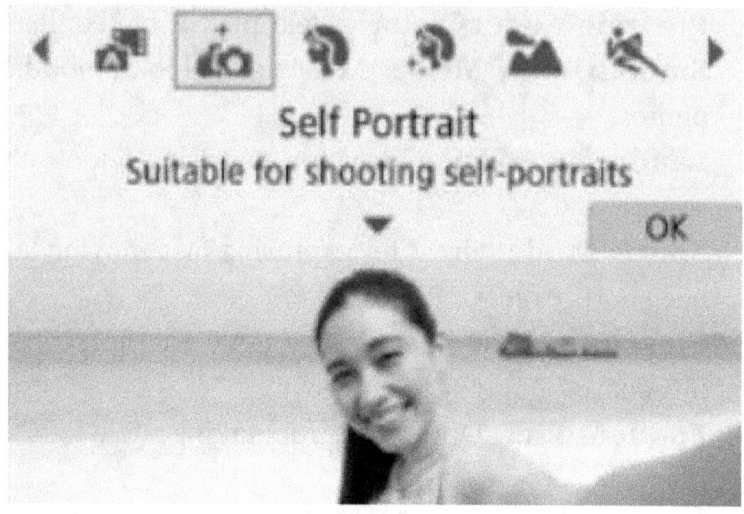

Adjust how bright the picture is and make your skin look smoother. You can choose from five levels for both brightness and skin smoothness. You can also blur the background by adjusting the background level. To take a photo, press the shutter button or tap the screen if Touch Shutter is enabled. If you want to take selfies, rotate the screen towards you and tap the specified button on the lower left.

Portrait Mode
Portrait mode blurs the background, making the person in the photo stand out. It also makes skin and hair look smoother.

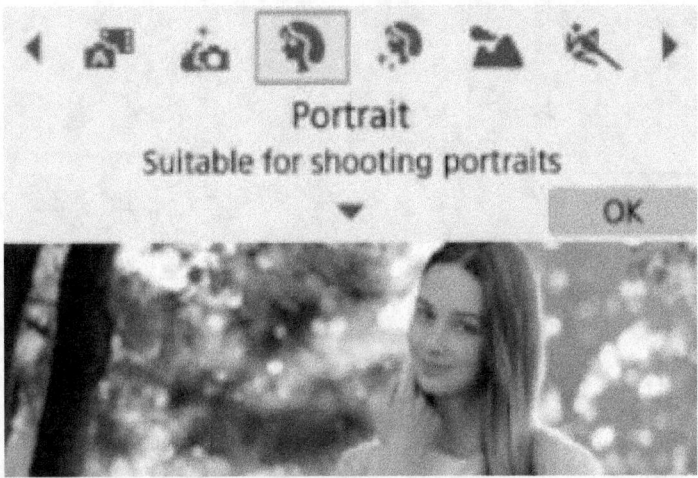

Choose a location where the subject is far away from the background. The more distance between them, the blurrier the background will be. This helps the subject stand out against a clean, dark background. Use a zoom lens, and if available, zoom in to frame the subject from the waist up.

Focus on the subject's face. Ensure that the AF point turns green on the face before taking the shot. If you're taking close-up shots of the face, you can enable "Eye Detection AF" for sharp focus on the subject's eyes. Capture multiple shots by keeping the shutter button pressed down, especially if you want to capture different facial expressions and poses.

Smooth Skin Mode
Use the Smooth Skin mode to make your skin look nicer in photos. It uses image editing to make your skin appear smoother and more attractive.

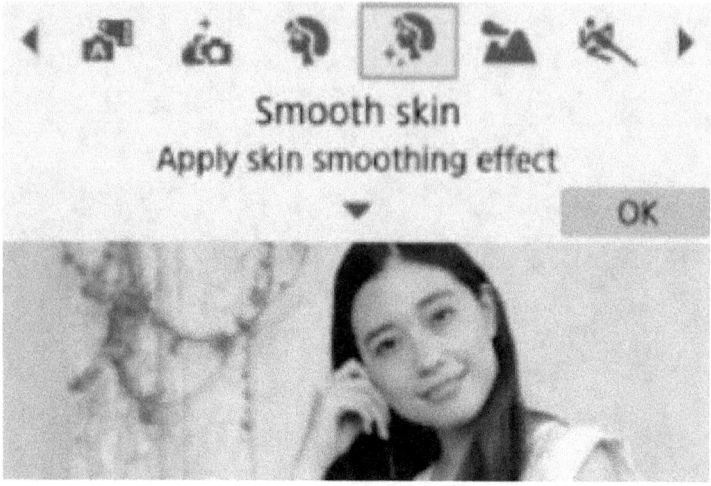

Smooth skin
Apply skin smoothing effect

OK

Turn on face detection in the camera settings. Look for frames around the main subjects, which help with skin smoothing. To make skin smoothing more effective, adjust your distance to ensure the frame appears on the subject's face. Focus on the face, making sure the AF point turns green before taking the shot. For close-ups of the face, you can enable "Eye Detection AF" to ensure the subject's eyes are sharply focused.

Landscape Mode

Use the Landscape mode on your camera for wide, scenic views or when you want everything in focus, from close-up to far away. This mode makes blues and greens vibrant and your pictures sharp and clear.

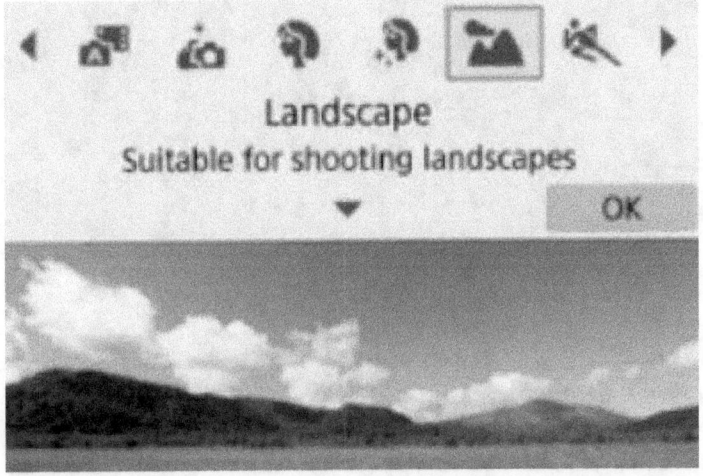

When you use a zoom lens, make sure it's set to the wide-angle setting. It helps objects both near and far to be in focus and makes landscapes look wider. Also, if you're taking pictures at night, keep the camera still. If you hold it in your hands, it might shake and blur the photos. It's better to use a tripod, a stand for the camera, to keep it steady.

Sports Mode

Use the [*] (Sports) mode to photograph moving things, like a person running or a car in motion.

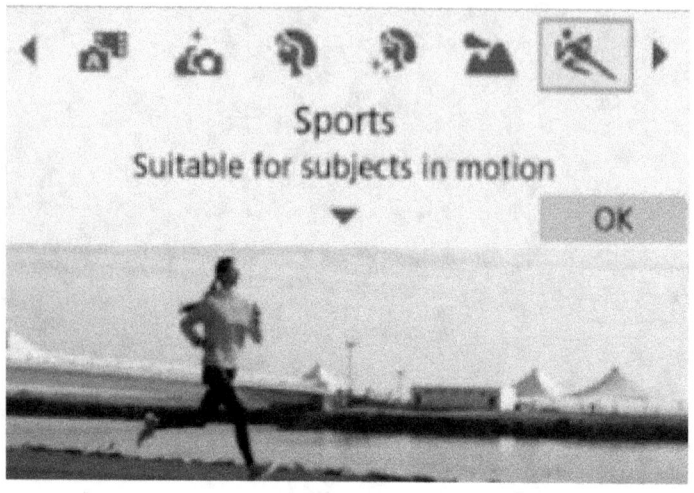

Use a zoomed-in lens. When taking pictures from far away, it's best to use a zoomed-in lens. Focus on your subject using the autofocus frame, indicated by a blue point. Ensure to press the shutter button halfway to track the subject. To capture continuous movement, hold down the shutter button and keep shooting.

Close-up Mode

If you want to take close-up pictures of flowers or small objects, use the Close-up mode on your camera. To make small things look even bigger, you can use a special macro lens, which you must buy separately.

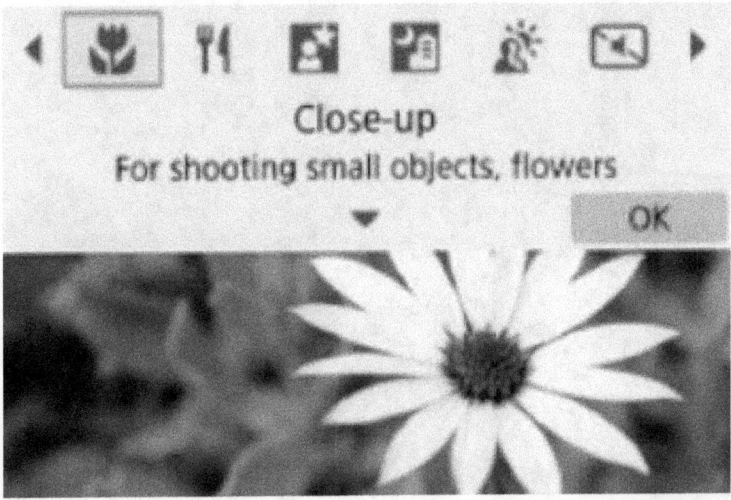

Use a plain background. It helps small things like flowers look better. Get close to the subject but not too close for the camera to focus. If you have a zoom lens, zoom in to make the subject look bigger.

Food Mode

To take good food photos, use the Food mode on your camera. It makes your pictures bright and tasty-looking. Plus, it helps reduce any reddish tint caused by certain lights.

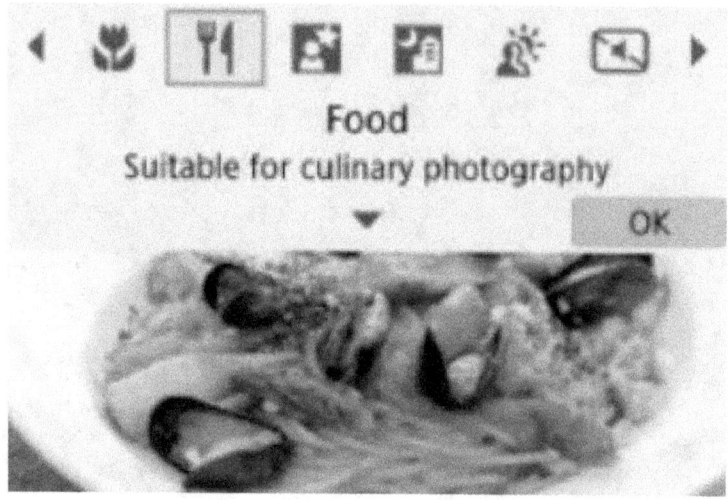

You can adjust the color tone of your food photos. If the food appears too reddish, move the setting towards "Cool" to reduce the redness. If you want to enhance the reddish tones, shift it towards "Warm."

Night Portrait Mode

To take pictures of people at night with a natural background, use Night Portrait mode. You need a flash, and it's best to use a tripod.

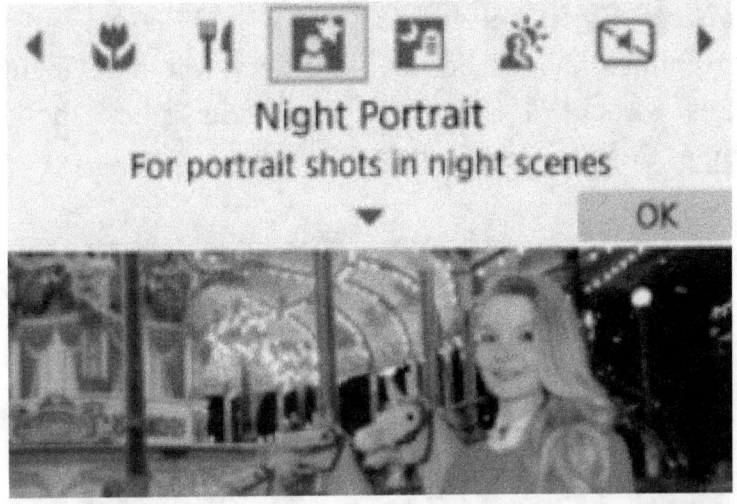

Night Portrait
For portrait shots in night scenes

OK

Shooting Tips

- Use a lens that captures a wide view and put your camera on a stand so it stays still.
- After taking a picture, look at it on your camera. If it's too dark, get closer to your subject and try again.
- If you have a zoom lens, zoom out to see a wider area at night.
- To prevent blurry photos, use a tripod to keep your camera steady, especially at night.
- Experiment with camera settings, including [A] mode, especially for night shots.
- When you use the self-timer and flash, a small light will flash to indicate the photo has been taken.

Handheld Night Scene Mode

The Handheld Night Scene mode lets you take nighttime pictures without a tripod. It takes four quick shots and combines them to reduce shaky pictures.

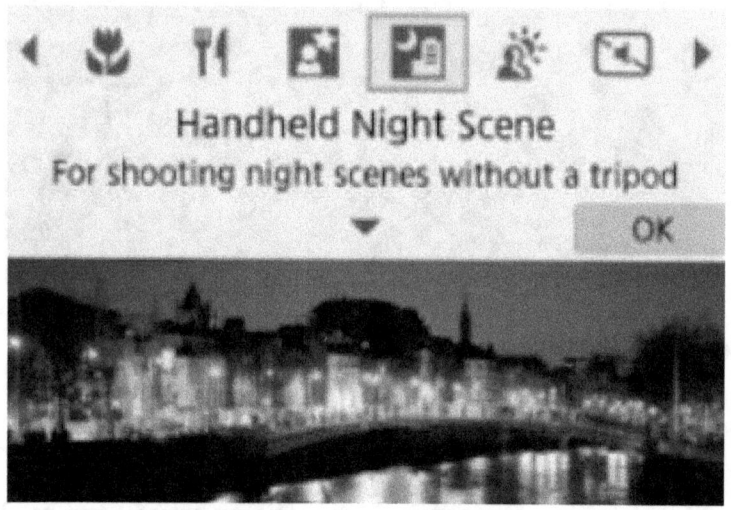

Make sure to hold the camera steady while taking pictures. In this mode, four photos are combined into one image. If there's too much shaking when you take the photos, they might not fit together correctly in the final image. So, keep your camera still.

HDR Backlight Control Mode

When you're taking a picture with both bright and dark areas, use HDR Backlight Control mode. It takes three shots at different exposures and combines them into one image. It helps capture a wide range of tones and reduces dark shadows caused by bright light in the background. HDR stands for High Dynamic Range.

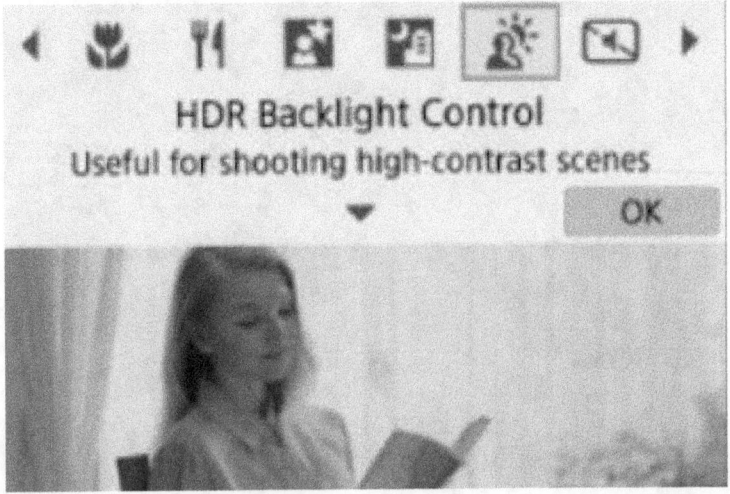

Be sure to keep a steady grip on your camera when taking photos. In this mode, the camera combines three shots into one image. But if there's too much shaking when you take the pictures, they might not fit together correctly in the final image. So, hold your camera still.

Silent Mode

When you need silence, you can take photos without any noise. Also, a white frame briefly appears on the screen while you're taking the photo.

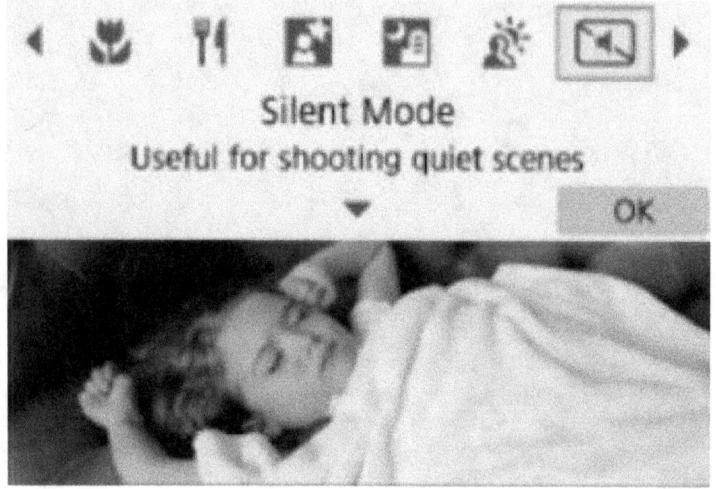

Before you start shooting, it's a good idea to take a few test shots. This is because you might hear some noise when the camera adjusts the lens aperture and focus, especially in certain shooting situations.

Creative Filters Mode

1. Choose creative filter mode.
2. Click the shooting mode icon.

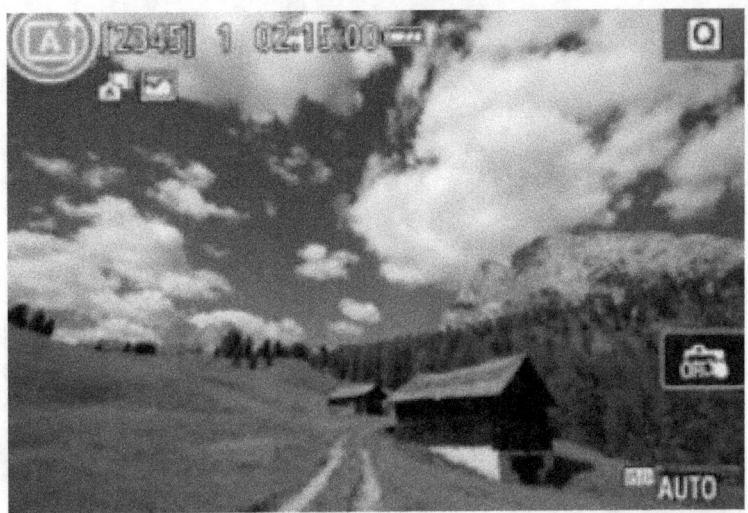

3. Pick a filter effect.

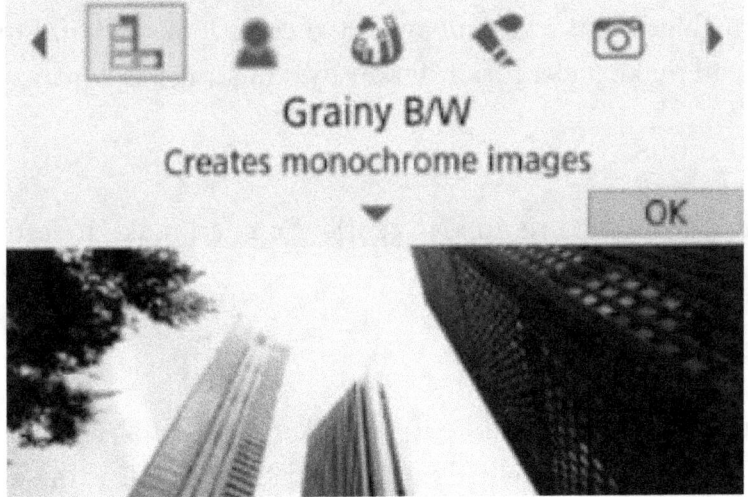

4. Adjust it the way you like, then take your shot!

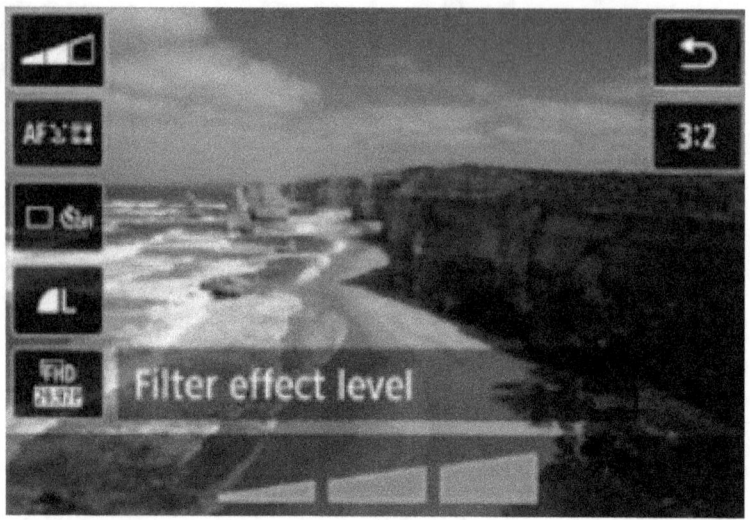

Creative Filter Characteristics

Grainy black and white means the picture looks old and fuzzy. You can make it clearer or darker by adjusting the contrast.

•Soft focus

It makes the picture appear gentle. You can make it softer or sharper by adjusting the blur.

•Fish-eye effect

It makes a photo look like it was taken with a fish-eye lens. It creates a curved effect called barrel distortion. How much the edges of the photo are curved depends on how strong the effect is. Be careful because it might blur the center of the photo if the quality needs to be higher. It focuses on the center using one point.

•Water painting effect

Turns a photo into a painting with gentle colors. You can adjust the effect to change color intensity. But, it might not work well for dark or night scenes; they might look uneven or noisy.

•Toy camera effect

Changes colors to look like toy camera photos and makes the corners of the picture darker. You can use color options to adjust the color tint.

• Miniature effect

It makes a 3D picture look. When you take a photo with the usual settings, the middle part looks clear. You can change which part looks clear (the focus area). It's best to use a specific focus method and align the focus point with the clear area you want in the picture.

• HDR HDR art standard

Photos show more details in bright and dark areas. When the contrast is low, they look like paintings with smoother colors. The edges of the objects might look bright or dark.

• HDR HDR art vivid

The colors are vibrant compared to HDR art standards, and the low contrast and smooth transitions make it look like a graphic artwork.

• HDR HDR art bold

The colors are very bright, making the main thing stand out, and the picture looks like a painting made with oil paints.

• HDR HDR art embossed

The picture's colors, brightness, and contrast are reduced to make it look dull and faded, like an old photo. The edges of the main objects in the picture will appear very bright or dark.

Miniature Effect Operation

1. Adjust the camera frame.
   - Use the frame to focus on a specific area.
   - To move the frame, tap the orange button or the heart icon.
   - Change frame orientation by tapping the icon on the left.
   - Use arrow keys to move the frame up, down, left, or right.
   - Center the frame by tapping the icon on the left.
   - Press SET to confirm the frame position, then adjust the focus point.

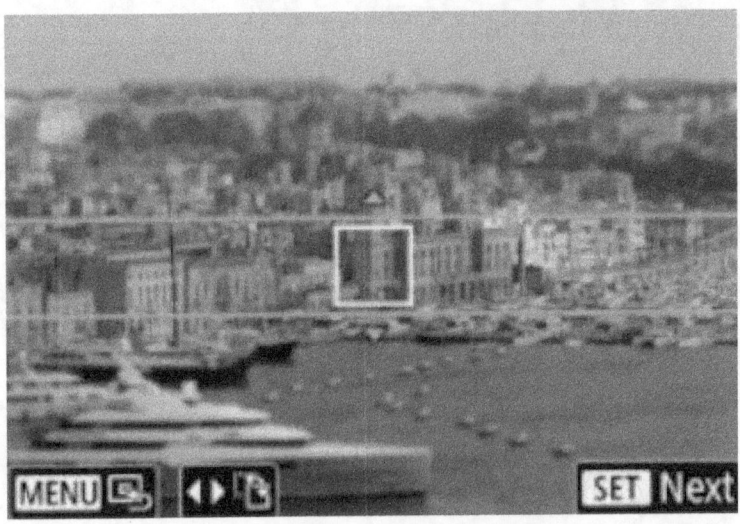

2. Change where the camera focuses:
   - Press the arrow buttons to move the focus point (it will turn orange).
   - Align the focus point with your subject.
   - Tap [] to center the focus point on the screen.
   - Press to confirm the focus position.

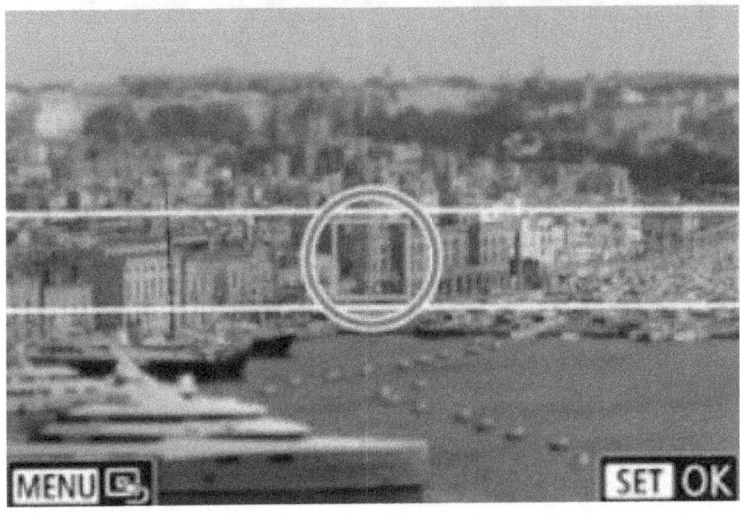

3. Capture the photo.

Choosing a Shutter-Release (Drive) Mode

You can choose how the camera takes pictures. There are two ways:

1. Single shooting: When you press the button, it takes one picture.
2. Continuous shooting: If you hold the button, it keeps taking pictures quickly until you release the button.

You can also set a timer for the camera to take pictures after a delay.

To take many pictures quickly (up to 135 shots), your camera needs a full battery, fast shutter speed, and wide aperture in a room at 23°C/73°F. The speed might change based on battery, temperature, settings, and lens type. Also, using certain features like Servo AF or when the camera's memory is full can make the speed slower.

Setting Resolution and File Type (The Image Quality Setting)

Image Quality setting

Choose how clear you want the picture to be and how many pixels it should have.

1. Pick the picture quality option.
2. Adjust the quality.

- For high-quality pictures, use RAW mode.
- For regular pictures, use JPEG mode.
- Press SET to confirm your choice.

Understanding file type (JPEG or Raw)

RAW Images

Raw images are like unprocessed data from a camera. They can be saved in two formats: RAW or smaller CRAW. You can edit these images using Digital Photo Professional software. You can adjust the images based on how you want to use them and then save them in formats like JPEG with the changes you made.

RAW Image Processing Software

To view RAW photos on your computer, it's best to use a program called Digital Photo Professional (DPP), part of EOS software. If you have an older version of DPP (Ver.4.x), it can't handle RAW images from this camera.

You need to update DPP to the latest version from the Canon website. Older versions like DPP Ver.3.x won't work either. Also, other software you buy might display something other than RAW images from this camera. You should check with the software maker to know if it's compatible.

CHAPTER 5: TAKING GREAT PICTURES AUTOMATICALLY

Adding Flash

Flash Photography

Using the flash is a good idea when you see the "I" icon on the screen, when you're taking pictures in the daytime with the sun behind your subjects, or when you're in low-light conditions.

1. Lift the flash using the flash lever.
2. Half-press the shutter button. Make sure you see a "flash" icon on the screen.
3. Take the photo. The flash will go off based on your flash settings.

After taking the photo, push the flash down with your fingers until it clicks back into place.

Flash Photography in [Av] Mode

The camera adjusts the flash brightness to match the setting you chose. In dim light, the main thing you're taking a picture of is well-lit with a quick flash, while the background is captured with a slow shutter speed. It helps both the subject and the background look good in the photo. It's better to use a tripod in these situations.

Flash Exposure Compensation

To change how bright or dark your camera flash is, follow these steps:

1. Press the Playback button on your camera.
2. Press the MENU button.

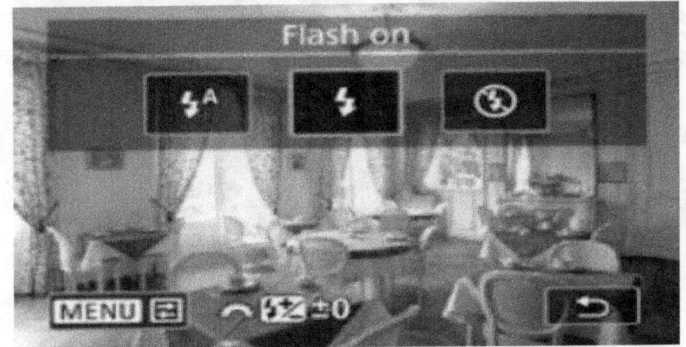

3. Choose "exposure compensation" from the menu.

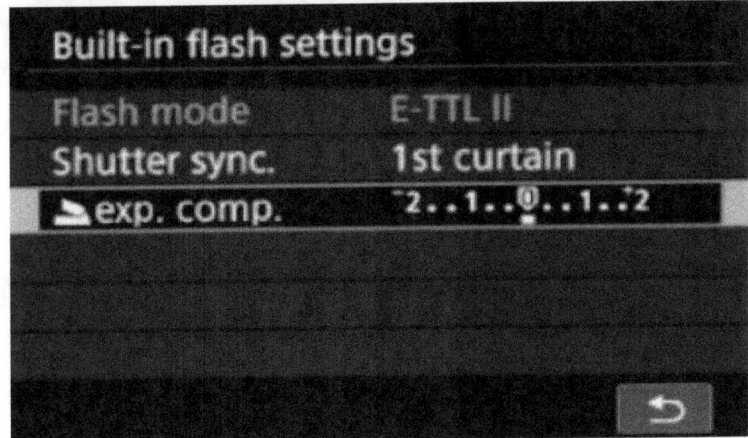

4. Adjust the compensation amount. To make the flash brighter, move it towards "Brighter." To make it darker, move it towards "Darker."

After taking your photos, follow steps 1-3 again to set the compensation amount back to zero.

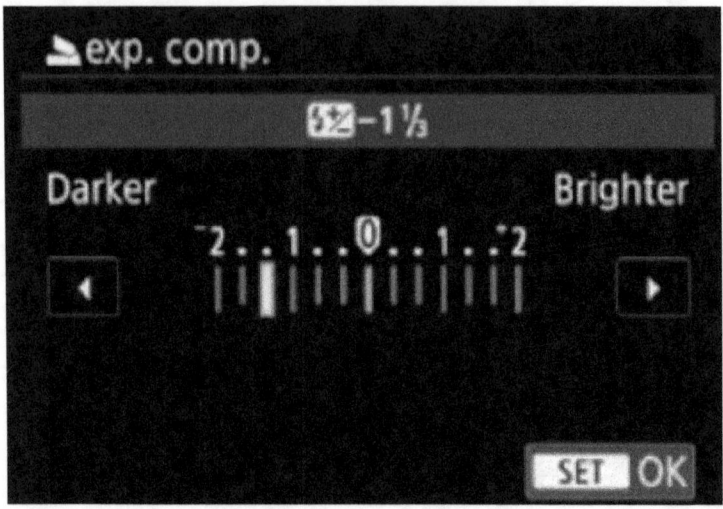

Even if you turn off the camera, the exposure compensation you set will still work. You can adjust flash exposure by turning the mode dial or using the built-in flash settings in the camera's control menu.

FE Lock

Shooting with FE (Flash Exposure) Lock ensures that the flash exposure is just right for the specific part of your subject you choose.

1. Raise the flash using the flash lever.
   Half-press the shutter button and check for the [flash] icon on the screen.

2. Focus on your subject.

3. Press the <*> button.
   - Center your subject on the screen, then press the <*> button.
   - The flash will emit a preflash to determine the necessary flash output.
   - If needed, you can press the <*> button multiple times to adjust the flash output.

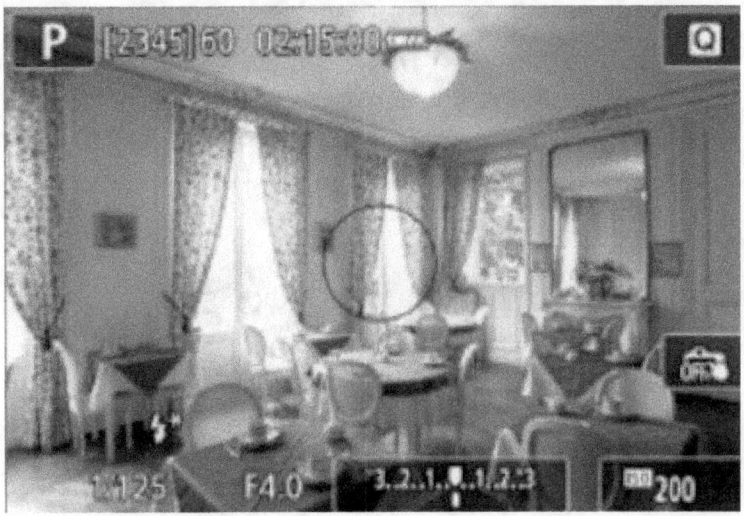

4. Take the picture by framing your shot and fully pressing the shutter button.

When the little lightning symbol blinks, your subjects are too far away, and your photos are too dark. Get closer to the subjects and follow steps 2-4 again.

Flash Control

You can adjust the flash settings on your camera using the menu:

1. Go to "Flash control" in the menu.

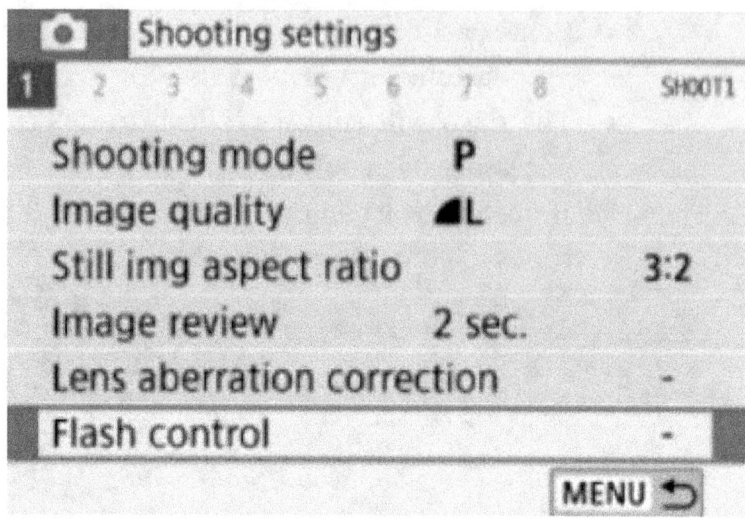

2. Choose the setting you want to adjust.

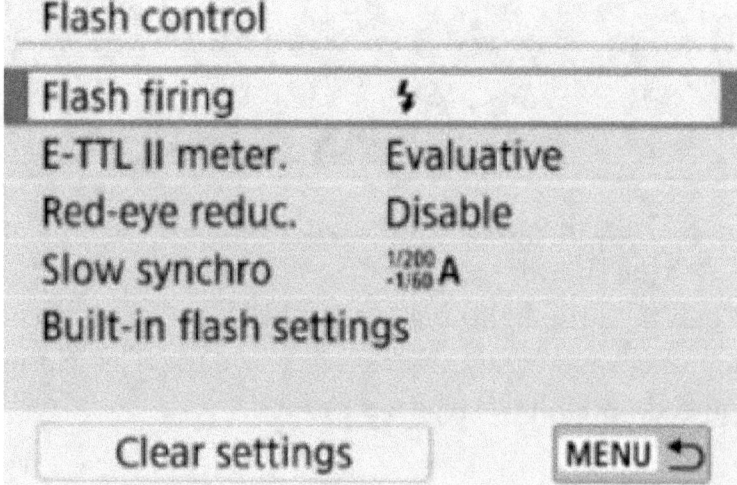

E-TTL II Flash Metering

For normal flash exposures, set it to [Evaluative]. If you set the "Average" option, the camera will calculate the flash exposure based on the whole scene, not just specific parts.

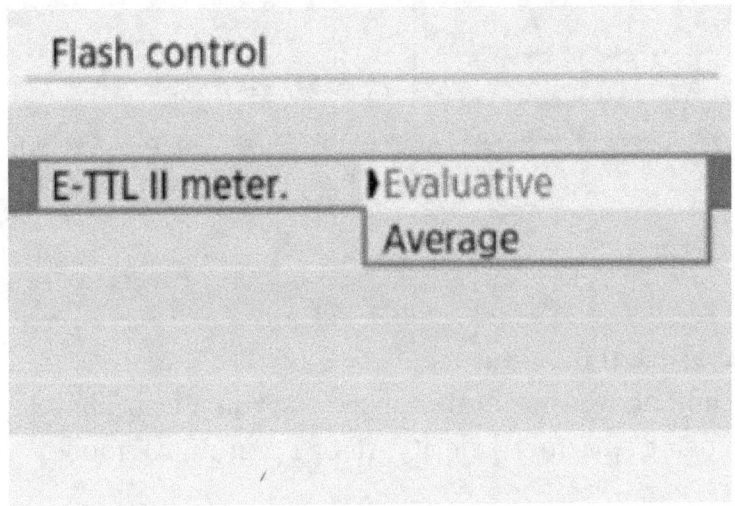

Using Red-Eye Reduction flash

Turn on the option to reduce red-eye. It makes a light flash before taking the picture to minimize the red-eye effect.

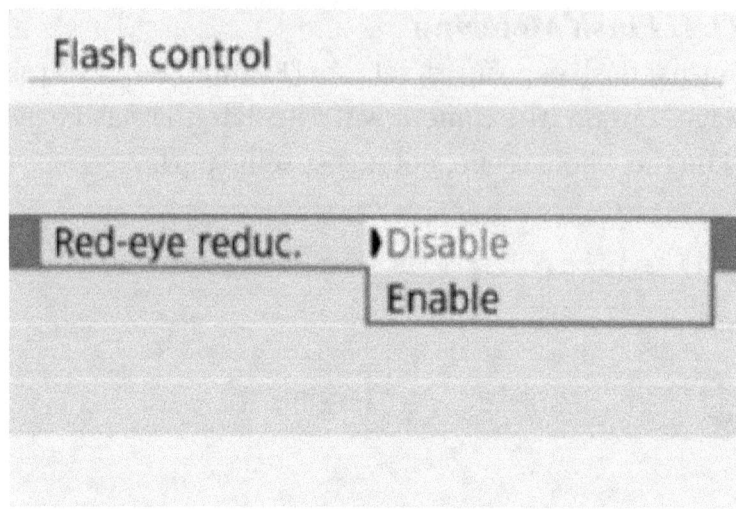

Slow Synchro

You can choose the shutter speed for your flash photography when using Aperture-priority AE or Program AE mode.

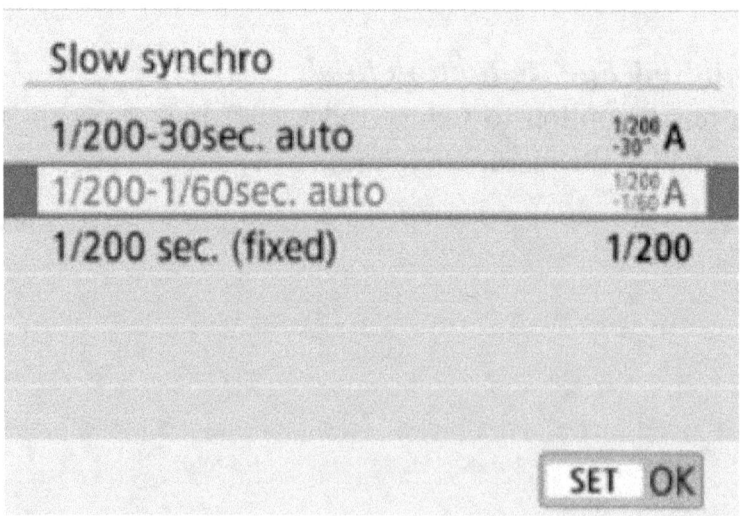

1/200-30sec. auto

The camera adjusts the flash sync speed automatically based on how bright the scene is. It can range from 1/200 second to 30 seconds. In low-light places, the camera uses slow-sync shooting and lowers the shutter speed for better photos.

1/200-1/60sec. auto

This setting stops the camera from using a slow shutter speed when it's dark. It helps avoid blurriness in your photos because of subject movement or shaky hands. But, be aware that when you use this setting with flash, the background might appear darker than you'd like.

1/200 sec. (fixed)

The camera's flash sync speed is set at 1/200 sec, which helps prevent blurriness in photos. But in low light, the background may appear darker compared to using a different setting between 1/200 and 1/60 sec.

Built-in Flash Function Setting

Select [E-TTL II] to use fully automatic flash mode. This means the camera determines the flash settings for you.

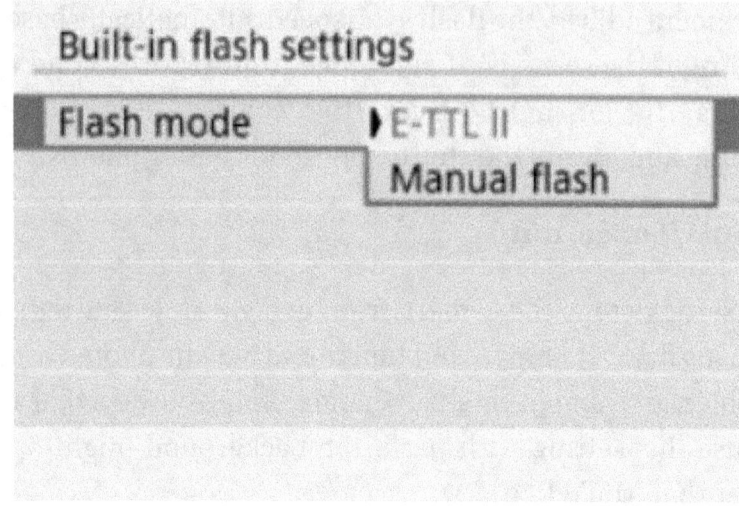

Choose [Manual flash] to have control over your flash output. You can select [Maximum], [Medium], or [Minimum] power settings. This option is available in [Tv], [Av], and [M] shooting modes.

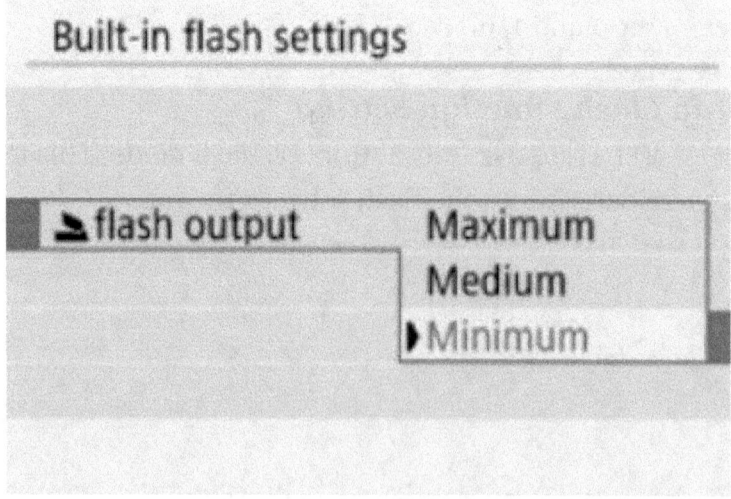

Clearing Built-in Flash Settings

1. Click on "Clear settings."
   Click "OK."

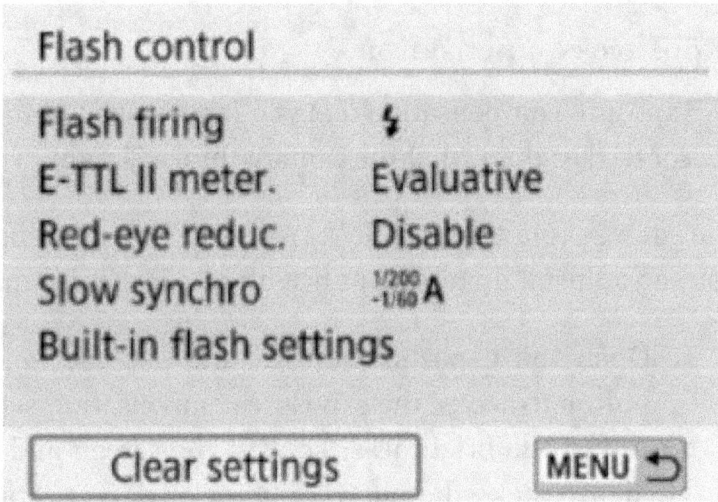

2. Now, the default settings are back to how they were.

Chapter 6: Taking Charge of Exposure

Introducing the Exposure

Exposure compensation

Exposure compensation lets you make your photo brighter or darker than what the camera thinks is right.

You can use it in the [P], [TV], [Av], and [M] shooting modes. You can adjust it up to 3 stops brighter or darker in small steps.

1. Open the exposure adjustment. Use the appropriate button to access the exposure compensation settings.
2. Adjust the brightness. Look at the screen and turn the dial to make the photo brighter or darker. You'll see a symbol like [Z] to show that you're making an adjustment.
3. Capture the photo. Once you're happy with the brightness level, take the picture.

If you want to go back to the standard brightness setting, just set the exposure indicator back to its normal position.

If you have the "Auto Lighting Optimizer" feature turned on, making your picture darker with exposure compensation might not work as expected. The image could still look bright. When you adjust the exposure compensation, it will stay that way even if you turn off the camera. It doesn't reset automatically. You can also adjust exposure compensation through the "Exposure comp." option in the camera settings.

ISO speed settings

Adjust the camera's sensitivity to light according to the brightness. In some modes, it's set automatically. To change it:

1. Tap the ISO icon.

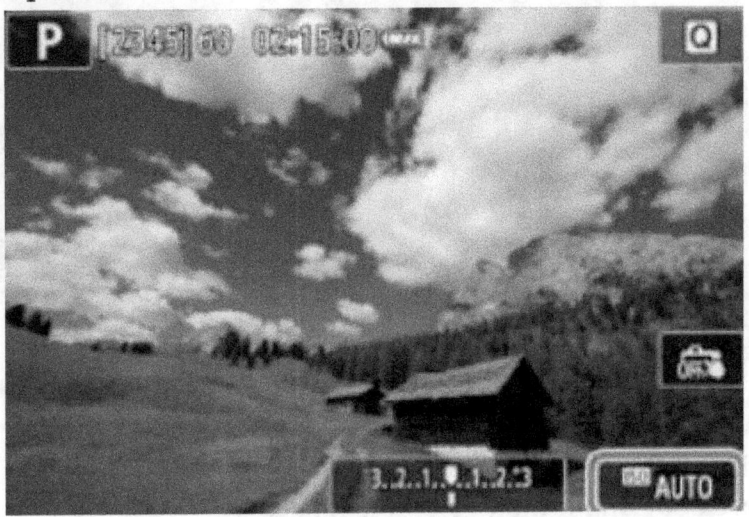

2. Use the left or right keys to adjust from ISO 100 to 25600. Or choose [AUTO] for automatic adjustment.

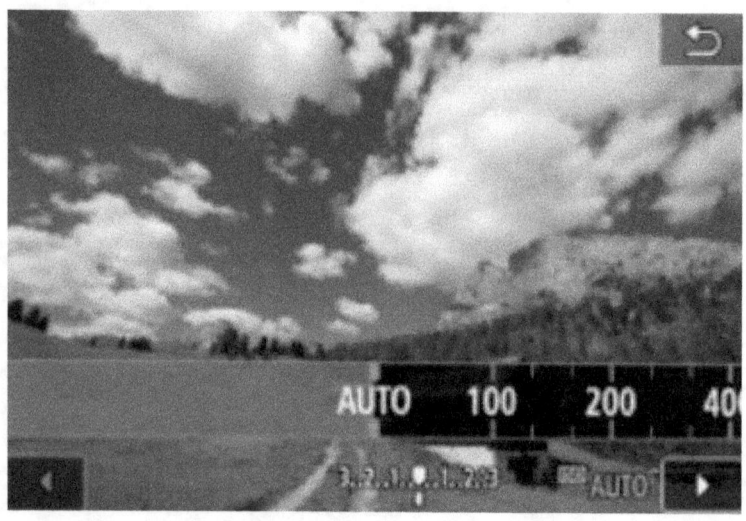

ISO Speed Guide

Low ISO makes pictures clearer but can blur or focus on a smaller area. High ISO helps in low light and focuses on a larger area but might make pictures noisy.

You can change the ISO speed settings in your camera. If you turn on ISO expansion, you can select a very high ISO setting (equivalent to ISO 51200), but it might make your photos noisy and less clear.

If you enable Highlight tone priority, you can't use the lowest (ISO 100/125/160) or highest (equivalent to ISO 51200) ISO settings. High ISO, high temperature, or prolonged exposure can make your photos look grainy or have strange colors.

In extreme conditions with high ISO, high temperature, and long exposure, your camera might not capture photos adequately. If you use a high ISO setting and flash for close-up shots, your photos might be too bright.

Max for Auto

You can set the highest ISO speed for automatic settings between 400 and 25600.

1. Choose ISO speed settings.

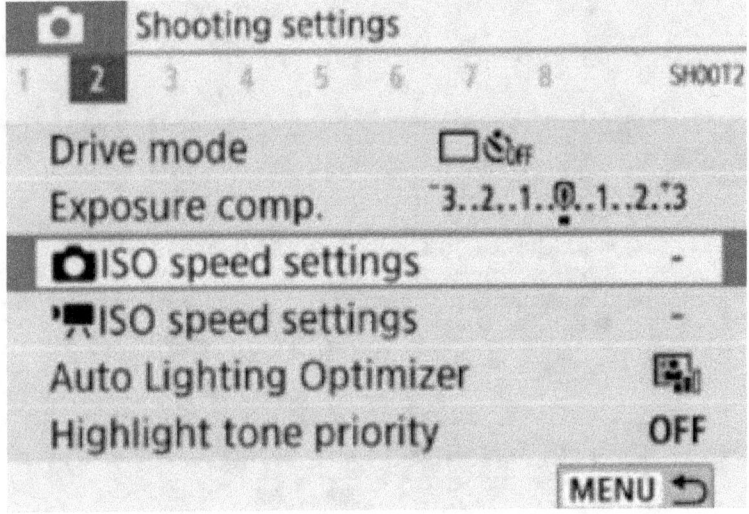

2. Pick "Max for Auto."

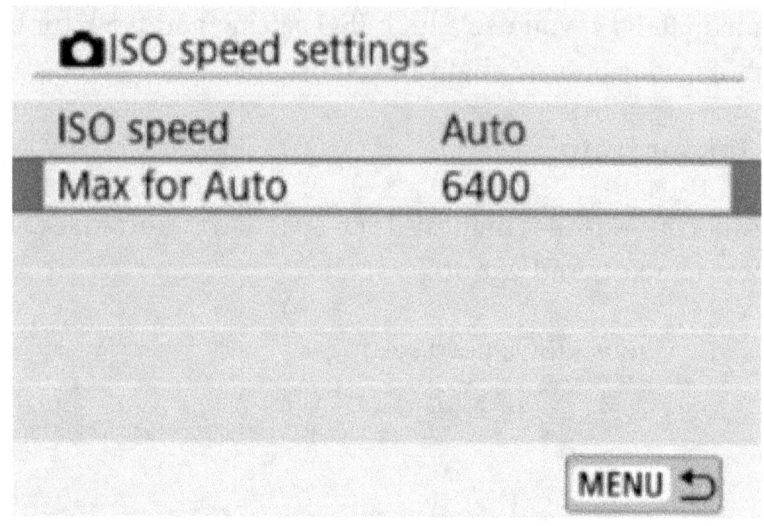

3. Decide the highest ISO speed.
   - Select the ISO speed and press SET.

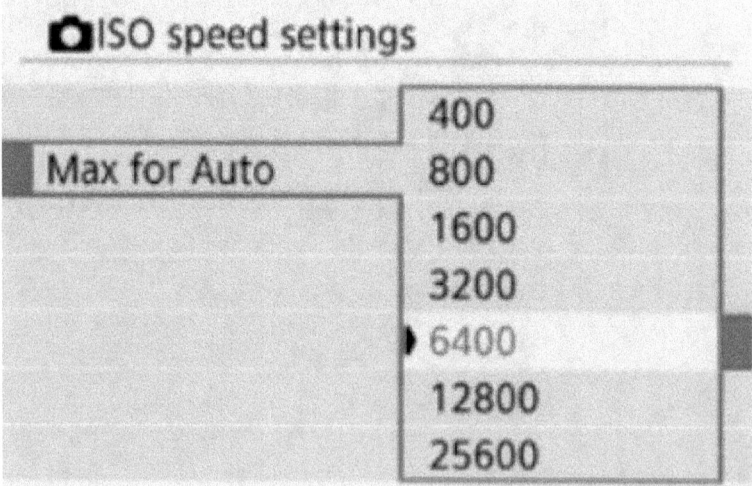

Exposure Simulation

1. Choose "Exposure Simulation."

2. Pick a setting.

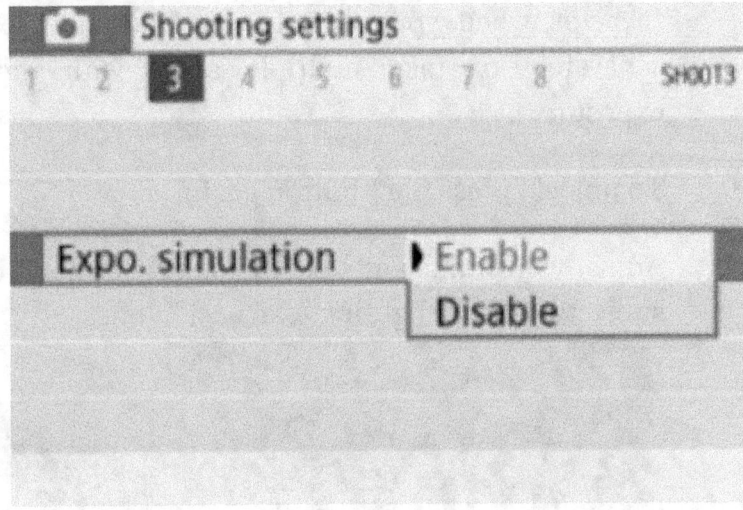

Enable (Exp. SIM)

When you adjust the brightness in a photo, it will look similar to how it appears in real life. If you change the exposure settings, the brightness of the photo will adjust accordingly.

Disable (DISP)

The picture is shown at a regular brightness level, making it easy to see. Even if you adjust the exposure, the picture stays at the regular brightness.

Exposure Lock (AE Lock)

1. Focus on what you want to take a picture of and press the shutter button halfway.
2. Press the * button.

You'll see a * icon, which means the exposure is locked. It helps when you want to set focus and exposure separately or take multiple shots with the same exposure.

To unlock, press the * button again.

3. Adjust your frame and take the picture. It helps capture subjects in tricky lighting, like backlit ones.

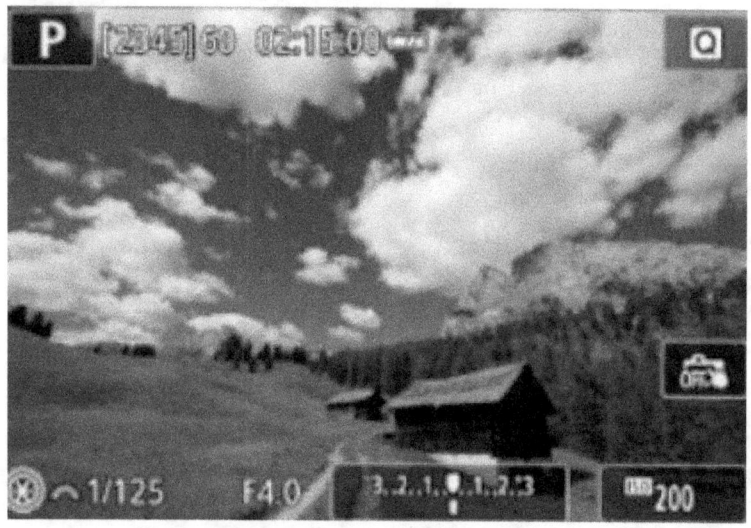

Metering Mode

1. Select [Metering mode].

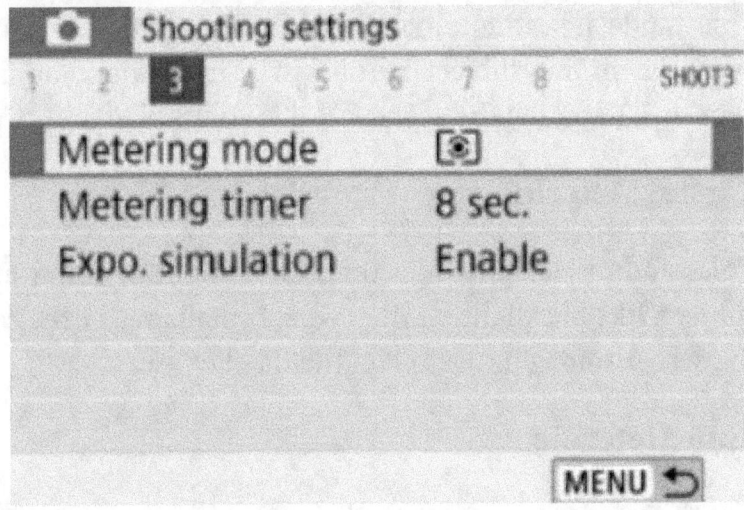

2. Set the metering mode.

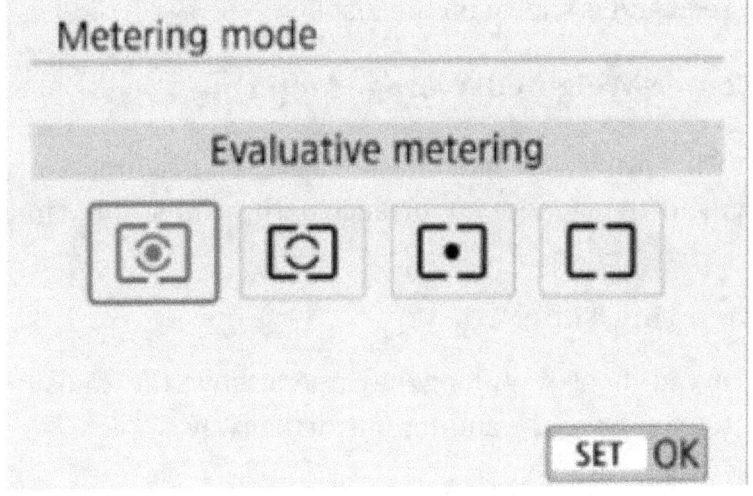

When taking pictures, you can choose how the camera measures the subject's brightness. You can choose from the four methods it has:

Evaluative Metering

This mode is automatic and works well for most situations, even when the subject is backlit. The camera adjusts the exposure to match the scene.

Partial Metering

This mode is useful when there are bright lights around the subject, like backlighting. It covers a small area at the center of the screen and is indicated on the display.

Spot Metering

Use this mode to measure the brightness of a specific part of the subject or scene. It covers a very small area at the center of the screen and is shown on the display.

Center-Weighted Average Metering

In this mode, the camera averages the brightness across the screen, giving more importance to the center of the image.

Metering Timer

You can choose how long the camera shows the exposure details after you press the shutter button halfway.

1. Go to the Metering timer in settings.
2. Pick how long you want the details to appear.

Stepping Up to Advanced Exposure Modes (P. Tv Av and M)

Program AE Mode (P)

1. Choose the "P" mode on your camera, which means Program mode.

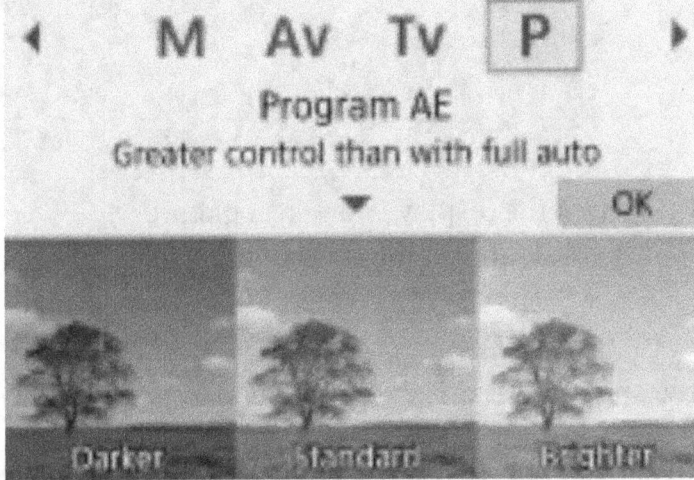

2. Focus on your subject.
   - Ensure the camera focuses on what you want to take a picture of. Press the shutter button halfway to do this.

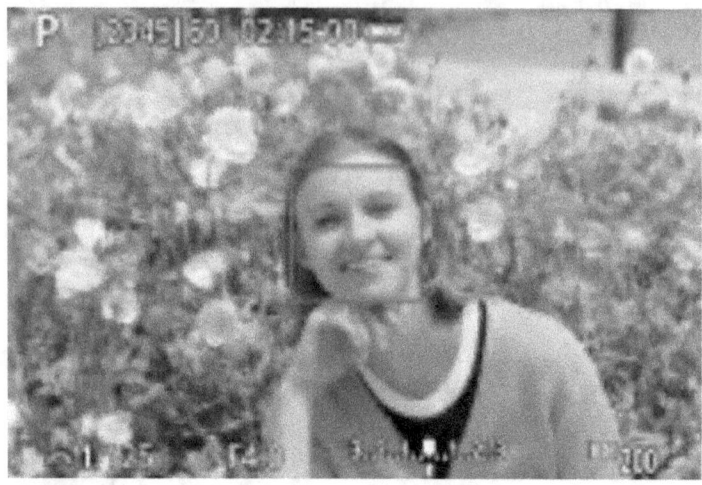

3. Check the display and take a picture.
   - If the numbers on the screen are steady, your picture will be just right.
   - If the numbers blink:

If the shutter speed is "30" and the f/number is the smallest, the picture will be too dark. You can make your camera more sensitive to light (increase ISO) or use a flash.

If the camera's shutter is fast (1/4000) and the aperture is wide open (largest f/number), the picture will turn out too bright.

You can make your camera less sensitive to light (lower ISO) or use a special filter to reduce light (an ND filter, sold separately).

Shutter-priority AE Mode (Tv)

In this mode, you choose how fast the camera takes a picture, and the camera figures out how much light to let in. A fast speed captures fast movements clearly, while a slow speed creates a blurry effect, showing motion. To use it:

1. Pick "Tv" mode.

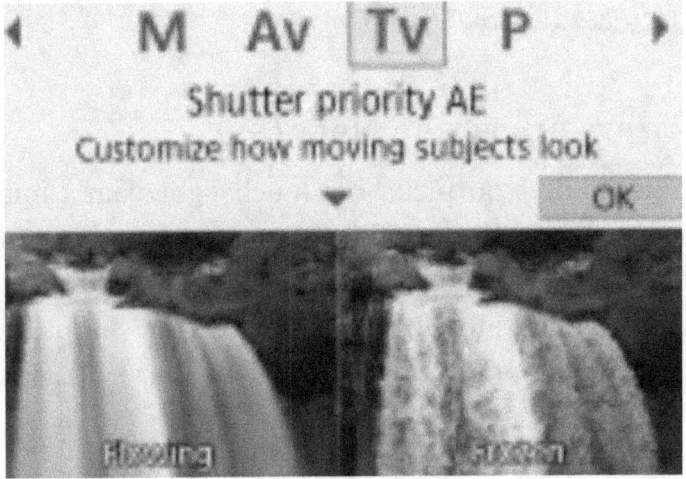

2. Select the speed you want.
3. Focus and press the button halfway.
4. If the display isn't blinking, take the picture for a standard exposure.

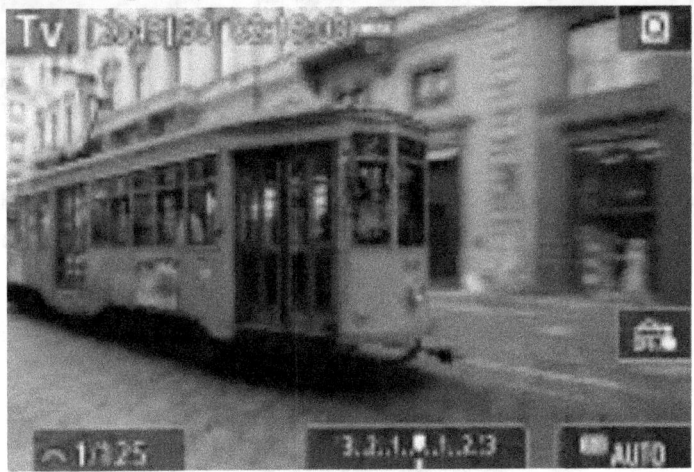

If your camera shows a low number blinking, it means the photo is too dark. Make the camera slower or increase the ISO.

If a high number blinks, it's too bright. Make the camera faster or decrease the ISO.

Aperture-priority AE Mode (Av)

In this mode, you pick how much light your camera lets in (aperture), and the camera figures out how long to keep the shutter open to make the photo look good. If you choose a higher number, more of the picture will be sharp. If you pick a lower number, only a small part will be sharp. To use this mode:

1. Choose "Av" mode on your camera.

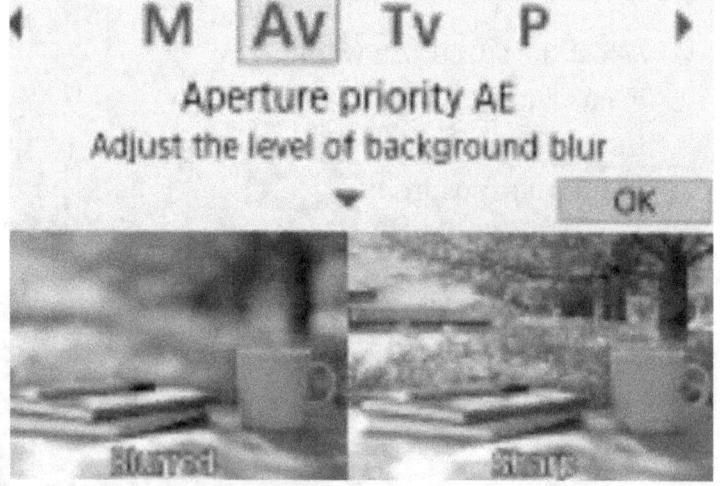

2. Pick the amount of light you want by turning the dial.
3. Focus on your subject and press the shutter button halfway.

4. Make sure the display isn't blinking, then take the picture.

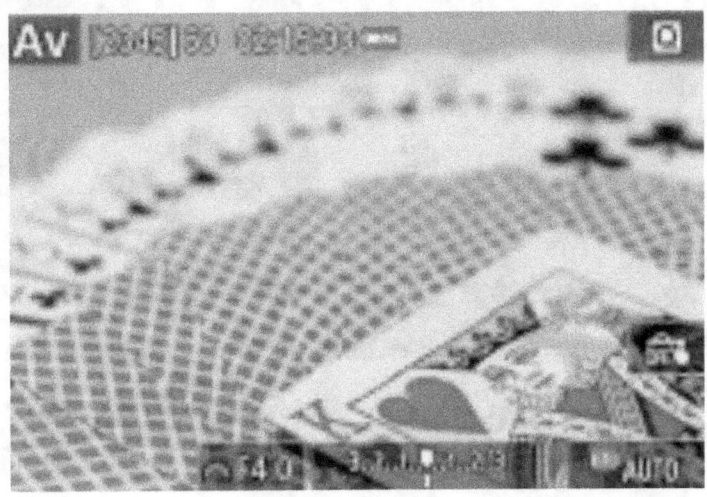

If you see "30" blinking on the shutter speed, it means your photo will be too dark. To fix this, open the aperture (set a lower f-number) or increase the ISO. If you see "1/4000" blinking on the shutter speed, it means your photo will be too bright. To fix this, close the aperture (set a higher f-number) or decrease the ISO.

Manual Exposure Mode (M)

In this mode, you choose both the shutter speed and aperture settings. To figure out the correct exposure, you can use the exposure level indicator on the camera or a separate exposure meter. "M" stands for Manual mode.

1. Choose Manual mode by setting the shooting mode to [M].

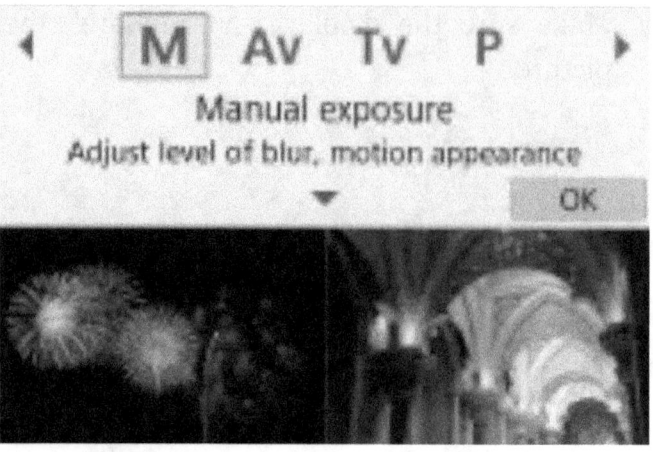

2. Select the ISO speed.

   If you use ISO Auto, you can also adjust the exposure compensation.

3. Pick your preferred shutter speed by turning the mode dial.

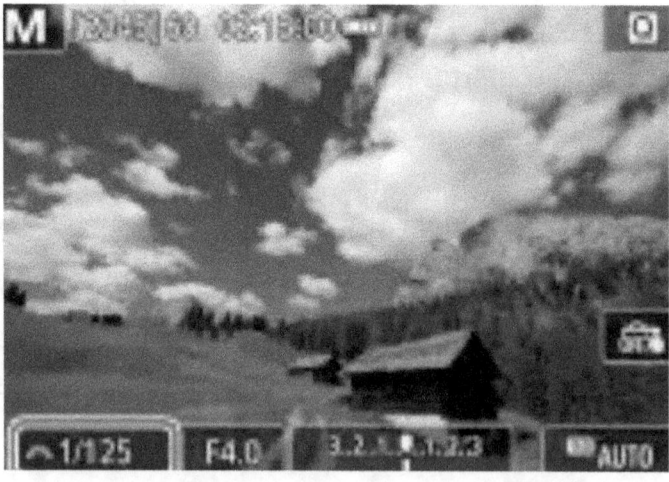

4. Set the aperture value.

Press the up arrow key, then turn the mode dial to choose the value you want.

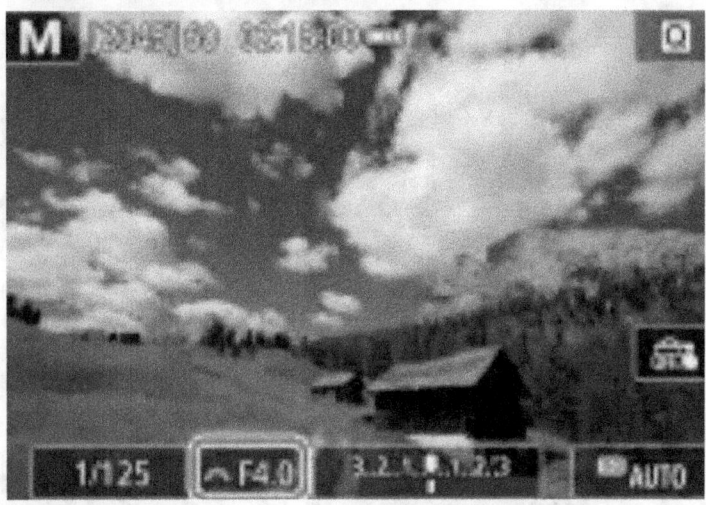

5. Focus on your subject by pressing the shutter button halfway.

   Check the exposure level mark to see if the current exposure level matches the standard exposure level.

6. Adjust the exposure settings based on the exposure level indicator, and then take your photo.

Long (Bulb) Exposures

In this mode, the camera's shutter remains open for as long as you keep the shutter button pressed, and it closes when you release the button. You'd typically use bulb mode for taking pictures of things like nighttime scenes, fireworks, the night sky, and other subjects that need extended exposure times.

1. Set the camera to manual mode ([M]).

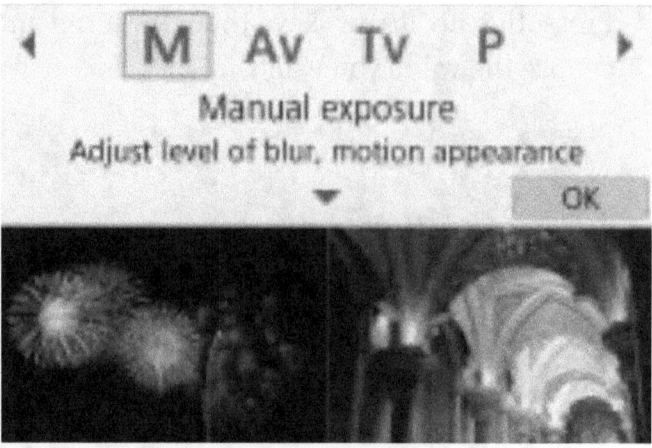

2. Choose the "BULB" option for the shutter speed. To do this, turn the mode dial to the left until you see "BULB."

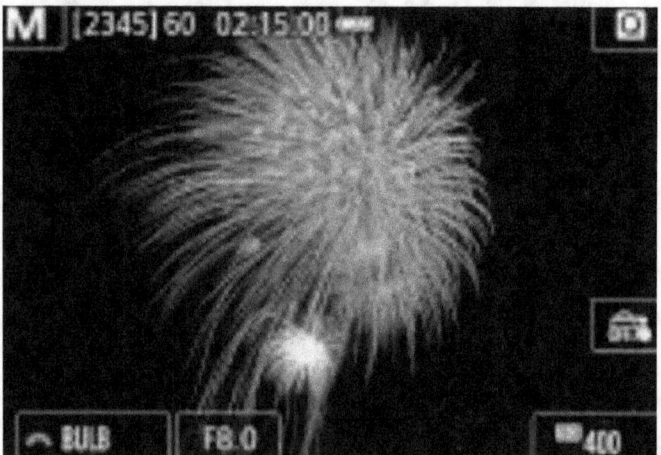

3. Pick an aperture value. Press the key to select it and turn the dial to adjust.
4. Take the photo. The exposure will last as long as you hold the shutter button down. You'll see the time on the screen to know how long the exposure has been.

Chapter 7: Movie Recording

Capturing Movies

Movie Mode

Autoexposure adjusts to the current lighting conditions. Here's how to use it:

1. Turn the shooting mode switch to "<k>."
2. Touch the shooting mode icon.
3. Choose Movie auto exposure. Press <SET>.

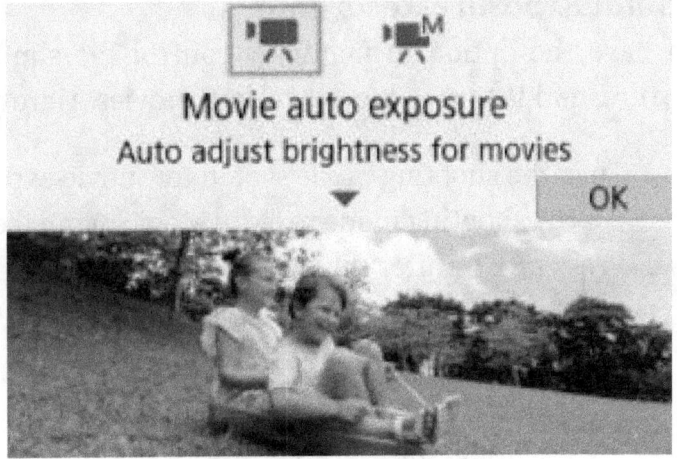

4. Focus on your subject. Use autofocus (AF) or manual focus before starting the movie. By default, "[z: Movie Servo AF]" is set to "Enable," so the camera continuously focuses. When you press the shutter button halfway, it focuses using the current AF method.

5. Begin recording your movie by pressing the movie shooting button. While recording, you'll see the "[oREC]" mark in the upper right corner of the screen. Sound is captured by the microphones at the marked positions. To stop recording, press the movie shooting button again.

Note: To keep the brightness level steady in your photos, press the <> button. Press it again to undo this. This setting stays until you press the <> button once more. You can adjust the brightness by up to ±3 stops. However, movie settings like ISO speed, shutter speed, and aperture value won't be saved.

Manual Exposure Recording

You have the option to manually control the shutter speed, aperture, and ISO speed for recording movies. Here's how:

1. Turn the shooting mode switch to "movie exposure."
2. Set the shooting mode to "M" (Movie manual exposure). Press <SET> after selecting it.

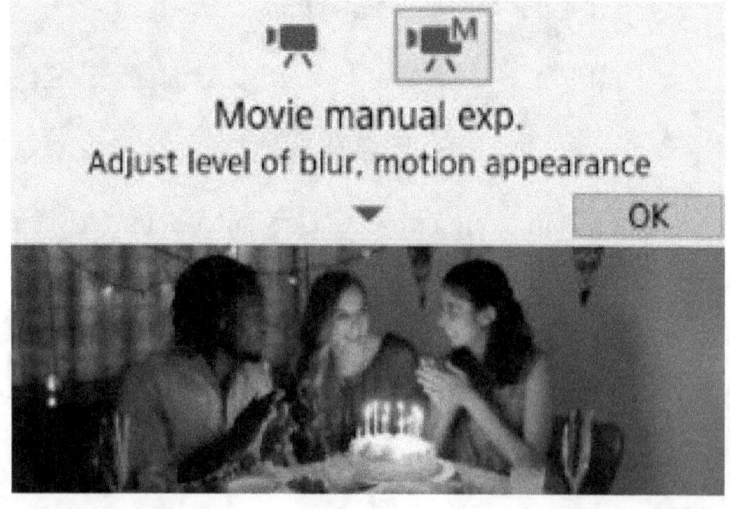

3. Adjust the ISO speed by tapping the ISO icon. If you're using ISO Auto, you can also set exposure compensation.

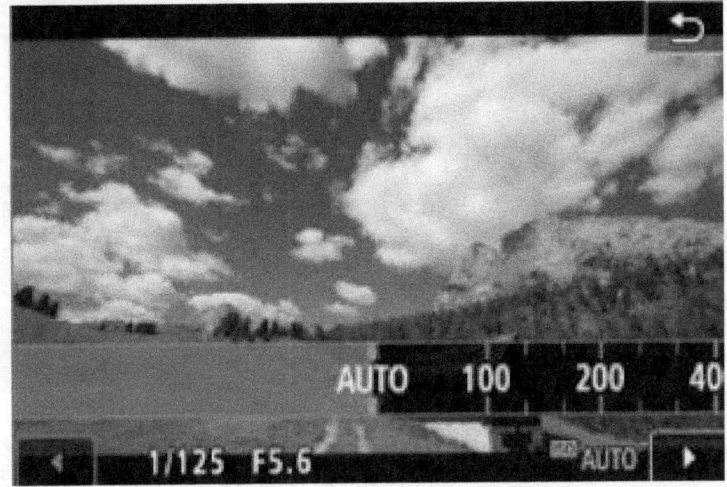

4. Set your desired shutter speed by turning the mode dial. You can choose a speed between 1/4000 and 1/8 of a second.

5. Select the aperture value by pressing the <W> key and then turning the mode dial to pick a value.

6. Once your settings are in place, focus your shot and start recording the movie. The process for focusing and recording is the same as in steps 4 and 5 for "[k] Autoexposure Recording."

Note:

- Recording 4K movies requires a high-performance card. For details, see "Cards that Can Record Movies".
- The maximum recording time per 4K movie is 9 min. 59 sec.

- Recording 4K movies greatly increases the processing load, which may cause the camera's internal temperature to increase faster or become higher than for regular movies. If [during movie recording, the card may be hot, stop recording the movie and let the camera cool down before removing the card. (Do not remove the card immediately.)

- From a 4K movie, you can select any frame to save as an approx. 8.3zmegapixel (3840×2160) JPEG still image to the card.

Movie Recording Quality

Choose the [Movie Recording Quality] tab, then pick [Movie Recording Size] to adjust your video's appearance. You can change the size, frame rate, and compression. The video will be stored as a type of file called MP4. The frame rate options depend on your [Video System] setting.

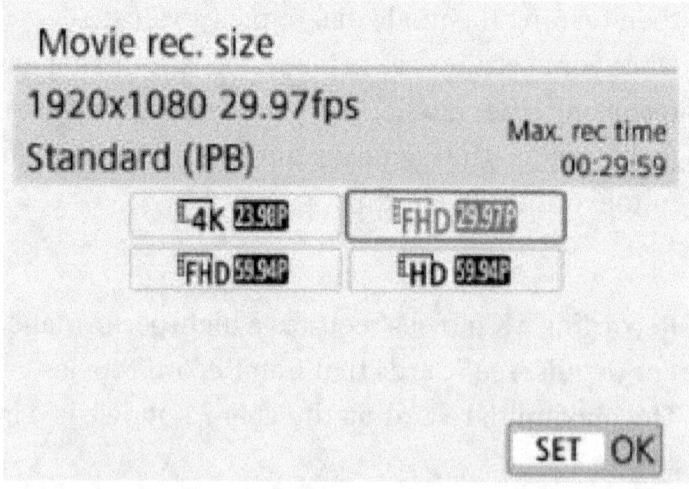

Image Size
[H] 3840×2160:

The movie is of really high quality, called 4K. It has a widescreen shape (16:9). You can only use this setting when the camera is set to record movies.

[L] 1920×1080:

The movie is in Full High-Definition, also known as Full HD. It has a widescreen shape, too (16:9).

[W] 1280×720:

The movie is in High-Definition, known as HD. It has the same widescreen shape (16:9)

Note:

If you change the video settings, adjust the movie recording size too. Some devices might need help playing 4K and L8/7 movies smoothly due to high processing requirements. The picture quality and background noise depend on the recording size, lens, and other settings.

Is this conversation helpful so far?

4K Movie Recording
When you're recording 4K movies, you need a high-performance memory card. For more information, check "Cards that Can Record Movies." The maximum time you can record in a single 4K movie is 9 minutes and 59 seconds.

Recording 4K movies puts a lot of strain on the camera, which can make it heat up faster than when shooting regular movies. If you see a message about a hot card while recording, stop recording and let the camera cool down before taking out the card. Don't remove the card right away.

You can also save any frame from a 4K movie as a high-quality 8.3-megapixel (3840x2160) JPEG image on your card.

Movie Self-Timer

1. Choose the "Movie Self-timer" option.

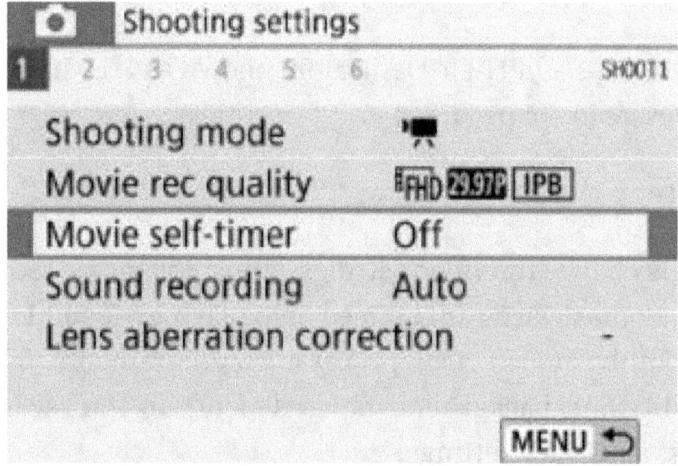

2. Pick a setting.

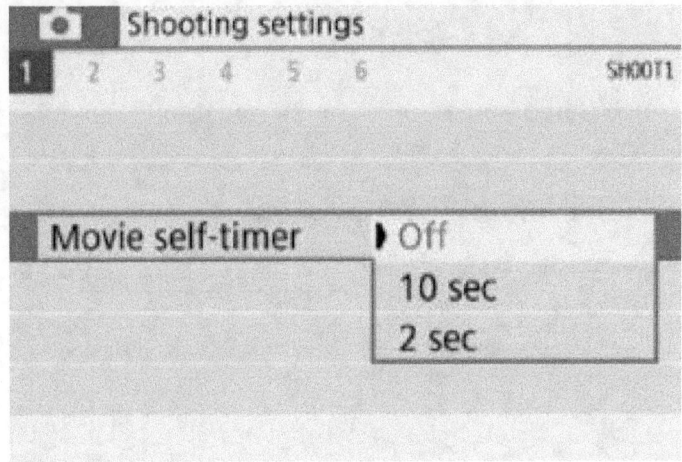

3. Start recording your video.

When you press the movie button, the camera beeps and shows how many seconds are left before recording begins.

Sound Recording

You can use the built-in microphone to record both movies and sound together. You can adjust the sound level as you like. To do this, go to the Sound recording settings.

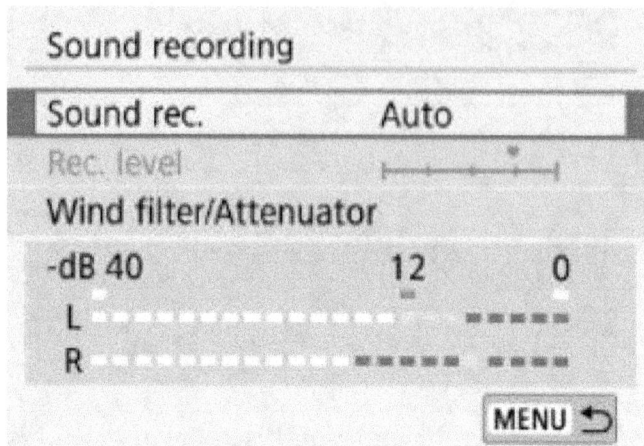

Sound Recording/Sound-Recording Level
Auto

The device automatically adjusts the sound recording level. It activates auto-level control in response to the sound level.

Manual

You can control how loud the sound is recorded. Go to "Rec. level" and use the left or right buttons while watching the level meter. Set it so that the meter sometimes touches the right side of the "[12] (−12 dB)" mark for the loudest sounds. If it goes over "[0]," the sound will get distorted.

Disable

No sound will be saved.

Wind Filter

Turn on [Auto] to make the wind noise quieter outside. It also reduces some low bass sounds when the wind filter is active.

Attenuator

Stops noise distortion from loud sounds. Even in Auto or Manual recording mode, loud noises can cause distortion. To prevent this, switch to Enable mode.

If you use Wi-Fi while recording with a microphone, there might be extra noise. It's better to use something other than Wi-Fi when recording sound.

The camera's microphone records camera noises when you're shooting. You can turn sound recording on or off in different modes. If it's on, the camera adjusts the sound level automatically. When connected to a TV, the camera's sound is heard unless you turn it off. You can't adjust the volume balance between left and right. The sound quality is 48 kHz/16-bit.

Time-Lapse Movies

When you take pictures at regular intervals, they can be combined to make a high-quality time-lapse video. A time-lapse video shows changes happening quickly, even though they took a long time in real life. This method is great for capturing things like changing landscapes, growing plants, or the movement of stars.

Here are the steps:

1. Choose a shooting mode on your camera.
2. Select "Time-lapse movie" from the menu.

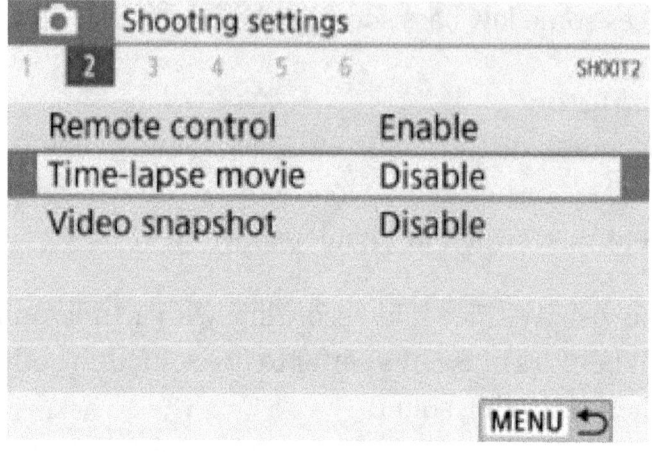

3. Choose the "Time-lapse" option.

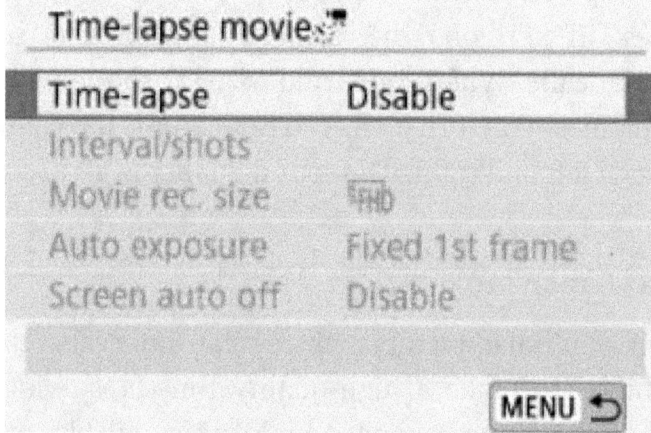

4. Choose a setting that matches the situation you're filming. If you want more control over how often the camera takes pictures and how many it captures, select "Custom."

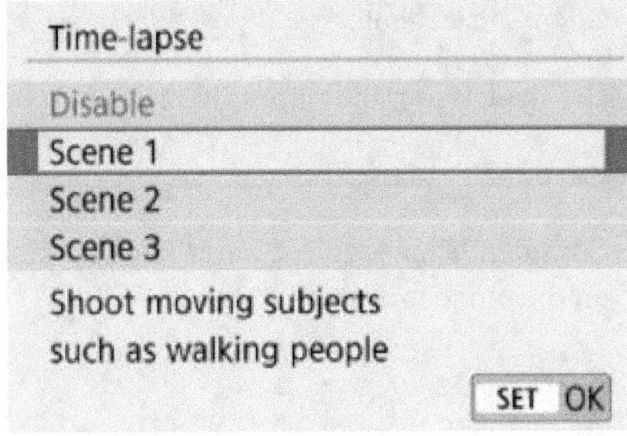

5. Adjust how often the camera takes pictures. Go to "Interval/shots."

   Choose "Interval (sec.)."

   Use the left or right buttons to select a time.

   Look at "Time required" and "Playback time" to decide how many shots to take.

   When [Custom] is set

   Choose the time interval by selecting "Interval" (in minutes and seconds).

   Press the "SET" button to show the options.

   Set the number you want.

   Press "SET" to confirm your choice.

6. Choose how many pictures you want to take.

Go to "No. of shots."

Use the left or right buttons to pick a number.

Press "SET" to confirm.

Consider "Time required" and "Playback time" to decide on the number of shots.

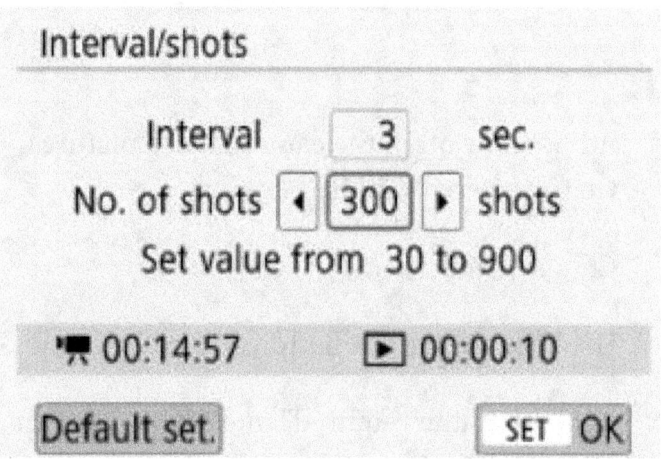

When [Custom] is set

Pick the digit you want to change.

Press "SET" to show your options.

Select the number you desire.

Press "SET" to confirm.

Make sure "Playback time" is not highlighted in orange.

Choose "OK" to save your setting.

Note: Depending on the scene you choose with "[Scene**]," you might have specific limits on how often the camera takes pictures and how many shots it can take. For example, if you set the number of shots to 3600, your time-lapse video will be around 2 minutes in NTSC and about 2 minutes and 24 seconds in PAL.

7. Choose the video quality you want:

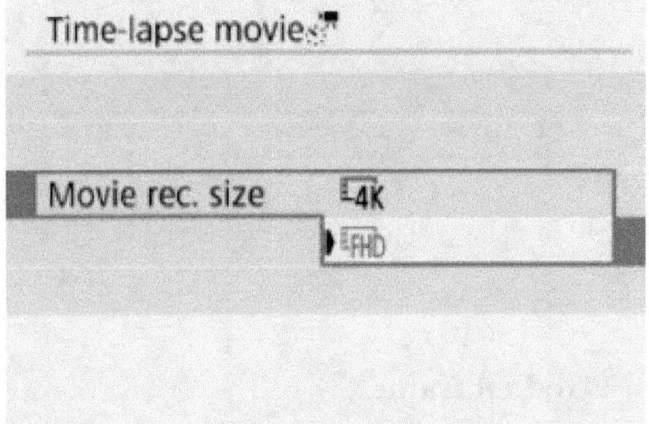

4K (3840x2160)

This records the video in very high quality with a wide screen shape. The speed of the video is 29.97 frames per second for NTSC and 25.00 frames per second for PAL. The videos are saved in MP4 format with ALL-I compression.

L (1920x1080)

This records the video in Full High-Definition (Full HD) quality. The video has a regular wide-screen shape. The speed of the video is 29.97 frames per second for NTSC and 25.00 frames per second for PAL. The videos are saved in MP4 (C) format with ALL-I compression.

8. Set up how the camera handles exposure:

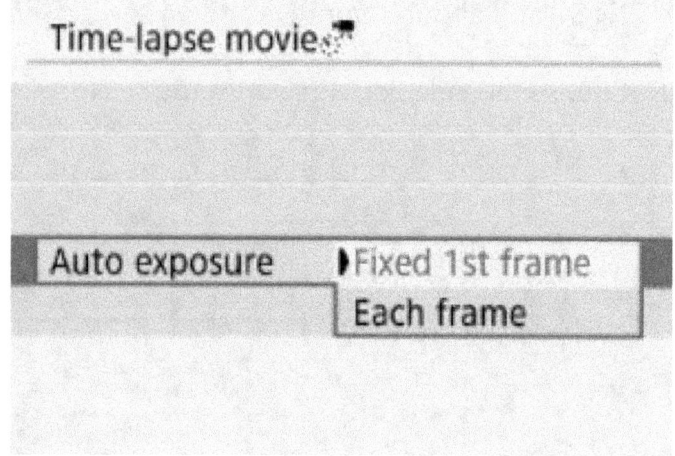

Fixed 1st frame

When you take the first picture, the camera will automatically adjust the exposure to match the brightness. This initial exposure setting will be used for all the following pictures. Any other settings you've adjusted for the first picture, like Picture Style and white balance, will also apply to the rest of the shots.

Each frame

With this setting, the camera adjusts the exposure for every single picture to match the brightness. If you've set functions like Picture Style and white balance to "Auto," they will be automatically adjusted for each picture too.

9. Set up the [Screen auto off] feature.

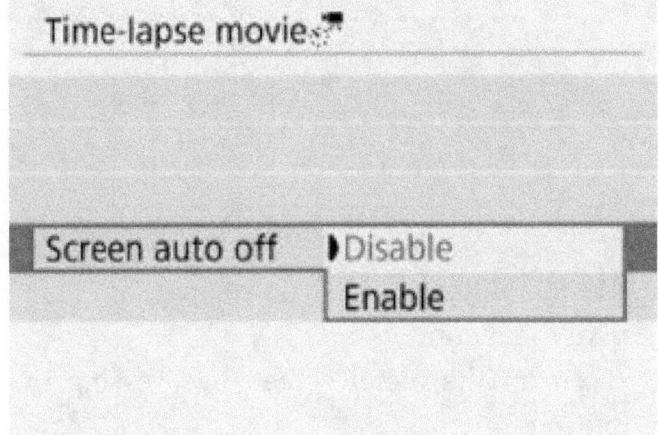

Disable

When recording a time-lapse video, you can still see the images as they are being recorded. However, the screen will turn off automatically after 30 minutes of recording.

Enable

The screen will go dark about 10 seconds after you begin taking pictures.

Note: While recording a time-lapse video, you can press the < B > button to switch the screen on or off.

10. Adjust the sound (beeper) settings.

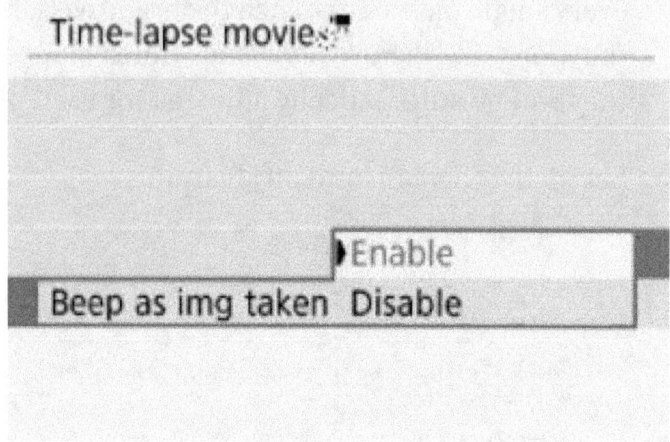

11. Review all the choices you've made.
12. Exit the menu.

    Turn off the menu screen by pressing the <MENU> button.

13. Make the time-lapse movie.

    First, press the shutter button halfway to make sure the focus and exposure are right.

    Then, press the "<o>" button to begin recording the time-lapse movie. You can see how many shots are left.

    While it's recording, you'll see "[REC]" on the screen. Autofocus won't work while you're recording a time-lapse movie.

    Because an electronic shutter is used, there won't be any clicking sounds when you take pictures.

When you've taken the set number of shots, the time-lapse movie recording will stop.

If you want to stop recording the time-lapse movie before it's done, change the "Time-lapse" setting to "Disable."

Note:

- If your memory card doesn't have enough space, it will warn you with an orange message. The camera can keep shooting, but it will stop once the card is full.
- If the movie file size goes beyond 4 GB and the card isn't formatted in exFAT, you'll see an orange message. If the movie file reaches 4 GB, the time-lapse recording will stop.
- Don't point the camera directly at very bright lights like the sun, as it can harm the camera's parts.
- You can't record time-lapse movies when the camera is connected to a computer or via HDMI.
- The continuous autofocus (Movie Servo AF) won't work during time-lapse recording.
- Avoid zooming the lens while recording a time-lapse; it can make the image blurry, exposure change, or lens correction not work correctly.
- Under flickering light, your time-lapse might have flickering, noise, or uneven brightness.
- What you see on the camera's screen might look different from the final movie, especially in low light.

- Moving the camera or capturing moving subjects might distort the image.
- Auto power-off doesn't work during time-lapse recording, and you can't change settings or play back images.
- No sound is recorded in time-lapse movies.
- If there's a big difference in brightness between shots, the camera may not stick to the set interval.
- If the camera can't take a shot at the scheduled time, it'll skip it, which can shorten the movie.
- If it takes too long to write to the memory card, some shots may not be taken at the set intervals.
- Even if you cancel time-lapse recording after one shot, it's still saved as a movie file.
- If you connect the camera to a computer using EOS Utility, set "Time-lapse movie" to "Disable."
- Image stabilization doesn't work during time-lapse recording.
- Time-lapse recording stops if you turn off the camera or change the setting to "Disable."
- Using a flash during time-lapse won't work.
- Two things will stop your camera from being ready for time-lapse movie recording and turn off this feature:
    - Picking "Basic settings" in the "Reset camera" menu.
    - Using the shooting mode switch to change your mode.

- Don't start time-lapse movie recording if you see a white "s" icon; wait for it to disappear to avoid reduced image quality due to high camera temperature.
- If you set "Auto exposure" to "Each frame," some shooting settings like ISO speed, shutter speed, and aperture may not show up in the time-lapse movie information in certain modes.
- It's a good idea to practice with test movies before making a real time-lapse movie.
- Both 4K and Full HD time-lapse movies cover the entire view. You can stop time-lapse recording by pressing the "<o>" button, and what you've recorded will be saved on the memory card.
- You can watch your time-lapse movie on the camera, just like regular movies.
- If it takes more than 24 hours but less than 48 hours to shoot, it'll show "2 days." For three or more days, it'll be indicated in 24-hour increments.
- Even if your time-lapse movie is very short (less than 1 second), it'll still create a movie file. It'll display "00'00"" for "Playback time."
- If you're shooting for a long time, it's recommended to use power outlet accessories (sold separately). The camera uses YCbCr 4:2:0 (8-bit) color sampling and Rec. ITU-R BT.709 color space for 4K/Full HD time-lapse movies.
- You can use the Wireless Remote Control BR-E1 (sold separately) to start and stop time-lapse movie recording.

Video Snapshots

Take quick video clips that are a few seconds each, and the camera will put them together to make a video album that shows the best moments of your trip or event.

1. Choose a shooting mode.
2. Pick "Video snapshot."

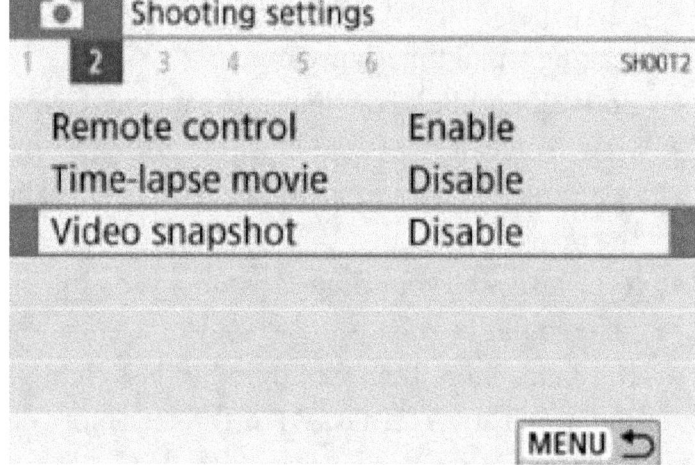

3. Select [Enable].

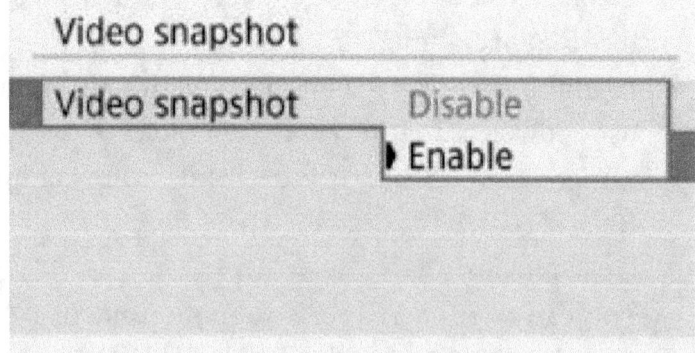

4. Go to "Album settings."

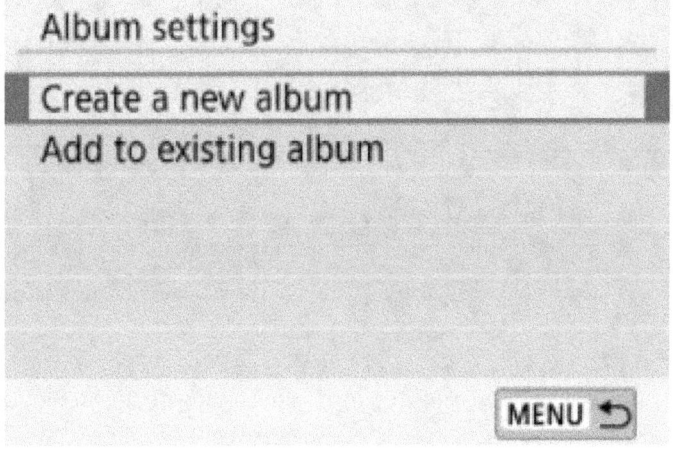

Video snapshot	
Video snapshot	Enable
Album settings	New album
Playback time	4 sec.
Playback effect	1x speed
Show confirm msg	Enable
Time required	4 sec.
	MENU ↺

5. Choose "Create a new album," then confirm by selecting "OK."

Album settings	
Create a new album	
Add to existing album	
	MENU ↺

6. Decide how long each video should play.

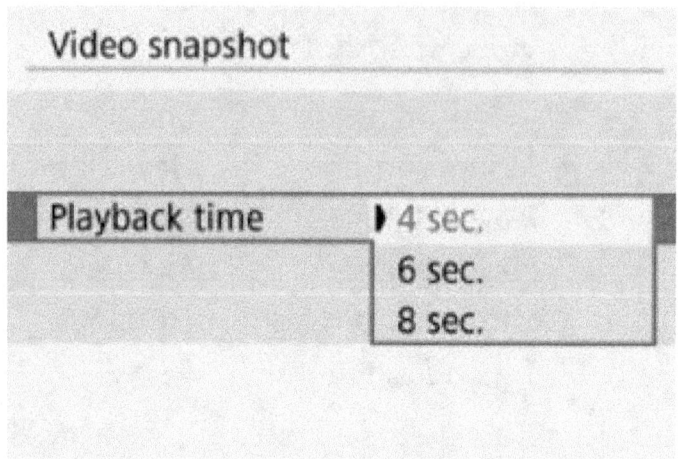

7. Select how fast you want the album to play.

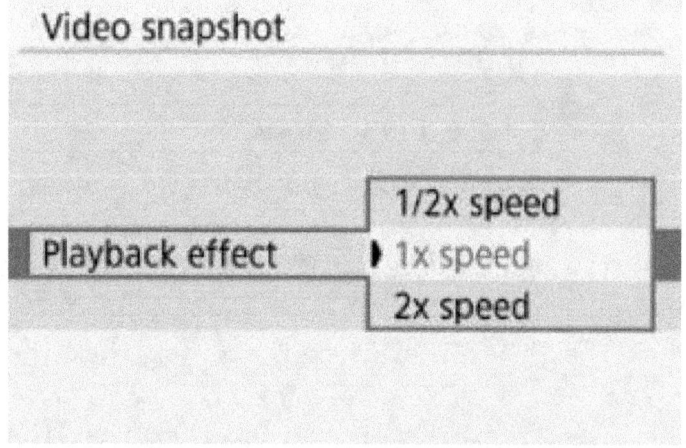

8. Check how much time you need to record based on your choices.

9. Close the menu by pressing the <MENU> button. A blue bar shows your recording time.

10. Start recording the first video snapshot by pressing the movie shooting button. The blue bar shows how much time you have left.

11. Save it as a video snapshot album by selecting "Save as album."

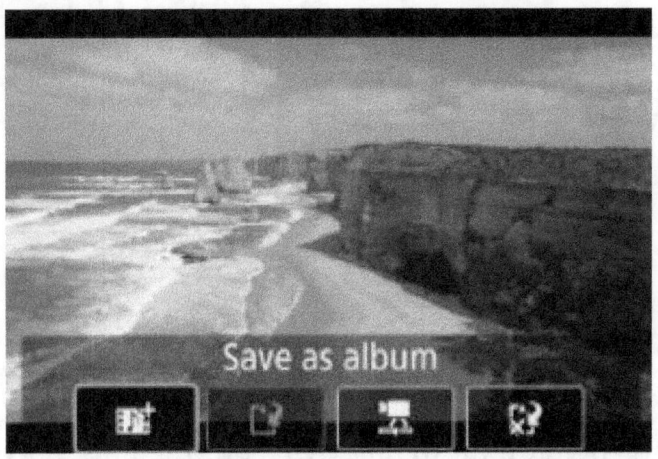

12. Record more video snapshots following the same steps. Add them to the album or create a new one.

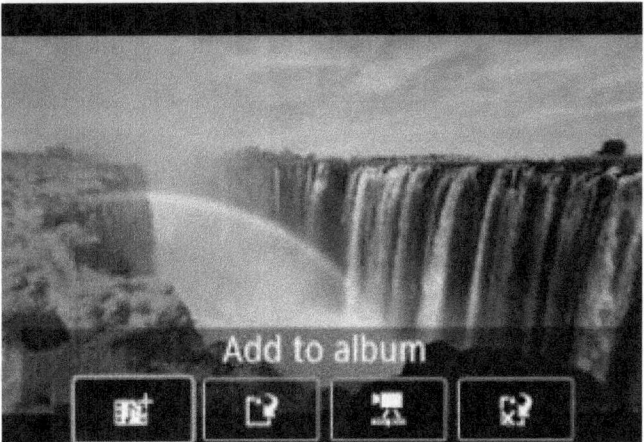

13. To stop recording video snapshots, switch "Video snapshot" to "Disable." To go back to regular movie recording, close the menu by pressing the <MENU> button.

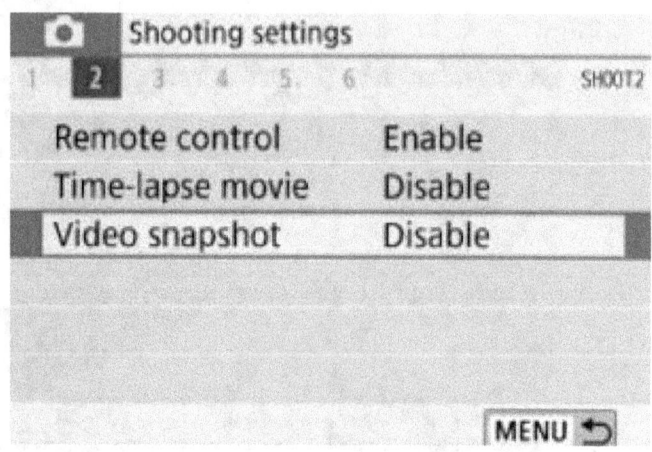

Note: If you want to quickly record the next video without a message asking for confirmation, turn off "Show confirm message" in the "Video snapshot" settings. This way, you can record the next video snapshot right away without any extra steps.

Adding to an existing album

1. Choose "Add to existing album."

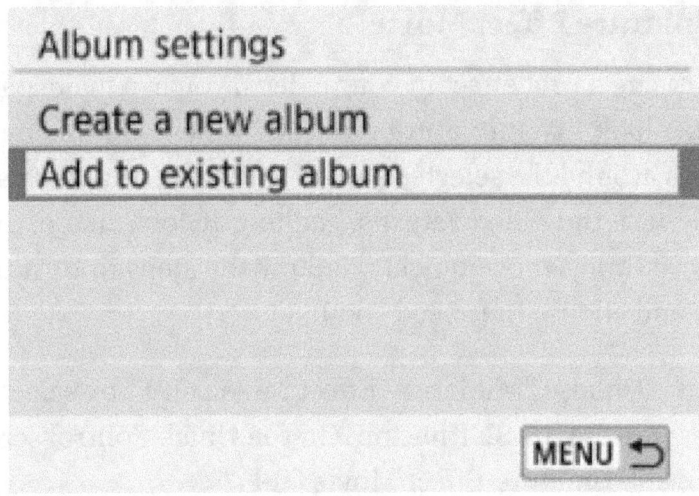

2. Pick an album using the left or right keys, then press <
   SET >. Click [OK]. Your video settings will match the
   chosen album.

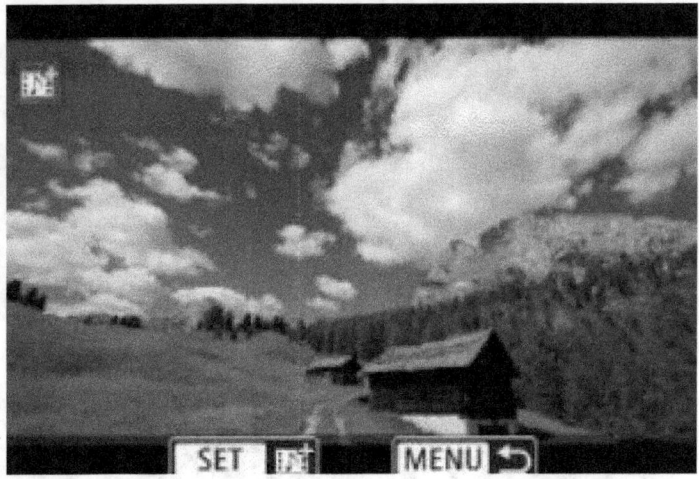

3. Close the menu by pressing the <MENU> button. You'll
   see the video snapshot recording screen.
4. Start recording your video snapshot.

Miniature Effect Movie

To create a cool effect in your videos, you can make parts of the video look like miniature models. You can do this by blurring areas around the selected part of the video. You can also choose how fast the video returns, making it look like a tiny world where things move quickly. Follow the steps to turn this effect on, and choose the speed you like!

1. Choose "Miniature Effect Movie OFF" by selecting it. Press the SET button. On the Quick Control screen, pick "Miniature Effect Movie OFF."

    You can also select "Miniature Effect Movie 5x," "Miniature Effect Movie 10x," or "Miniature Effect Movie 20x" as the playback speed.

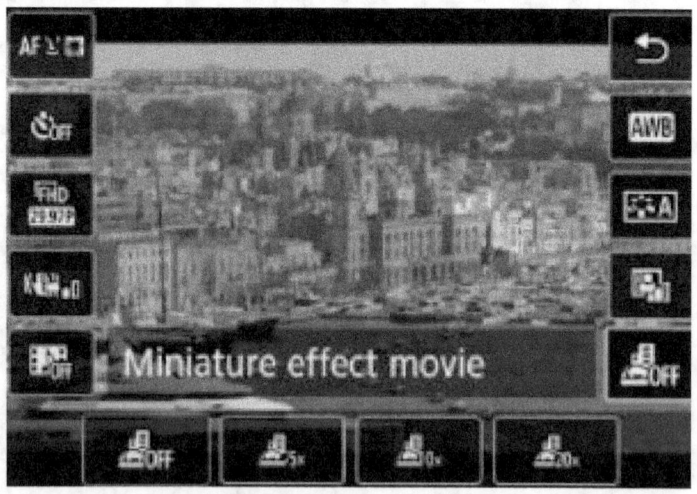

2. Adjust the frame that outlines the area you want to be in focus.

To make this frame moveable and show it in orange, press the "B" button or tap the "r" on the lower right of the screen.

If you want to switch the frame's orientation from vertical to horizontal or vice versa, tap "T" on the lower left of the screen.

To move a horizontal frame, use the up or down keys, and for a vertical frame, use the left or right keys.

After you've set the frame where you want it, press the "SET" button to confirm the position. Then, you can choose the autofocus point.

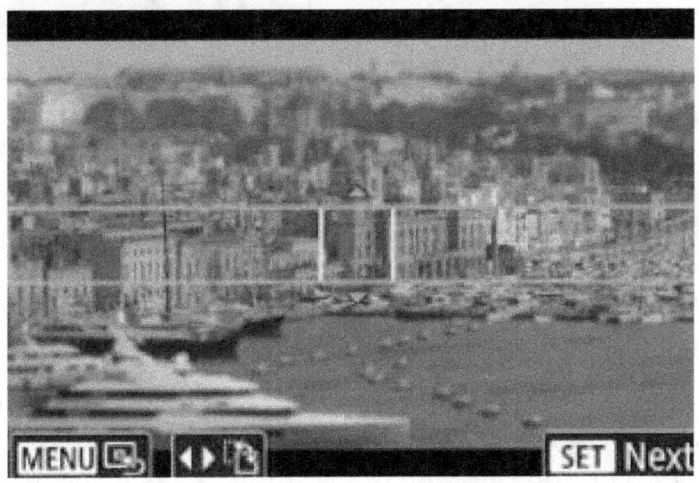

3. Change where the camera is focusing.
   The focusing point becomes orange and can be shifted.

   Use the arrow keys (V cross keys) to move the focusing point to the spot you want to focus on.

It's a good idea to have the focusing point match the outlined area.

After positioning the focusing point where you want, press the "SET" button to confirm the location.

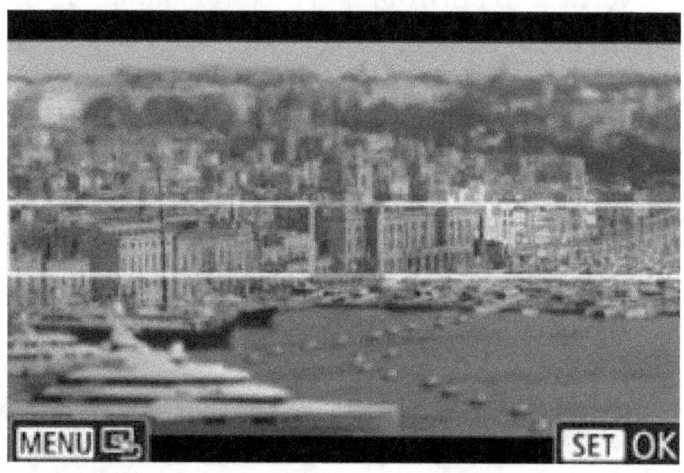

4. Capture the film.
   Push the movie recording button.

Movie Servo AF

When you turn this function on, the camera will keep focusing on the subject without stopping while you're recording a video.

1. Turn on the camera's continuous focusing during video recording.

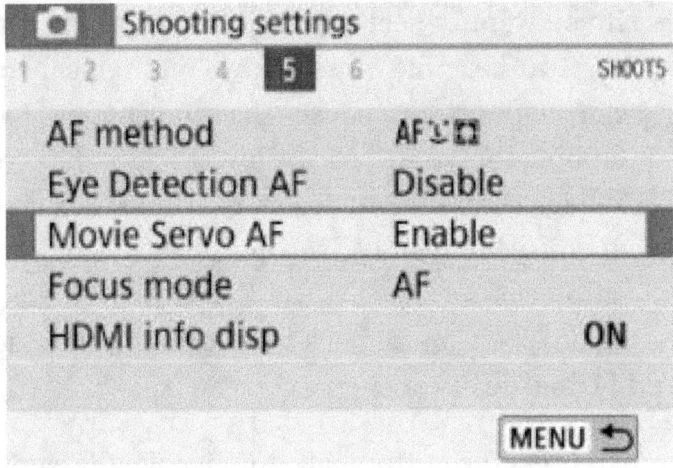

2. Choose "Enable" for the "Movie Servo AF" option.

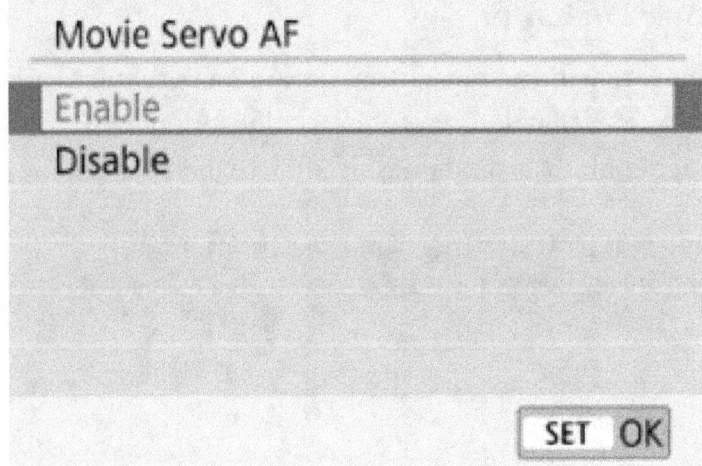

When [Enable] is set:

- The camera automatically keeps the subject in focus all the time, even when you're not pressing the shutter button halfway.

- If you want to keep the focus at a certain point or don't want to hear the lens making mechanical sounds, you can temporarily pause the continuous focusing by tapping [Servo AF] on the lower left of the screen.
- When you pause Movie Servo AF and then do things like opening the menu, checking playback, or changing the autofocus settings, Movie Servo AF will start working again when you go back to recording your video.

When [Disable] is set:

Ensure to press the button halfway to make the camera focus.

Movie Digital IS

When recording a video, the camera has a feature called "Movie digital IS" that helps reduce shaky footage. If your lens has Image Stabilization, make sure it's turned on.

1. Go to "IS settings" in the camera menu.

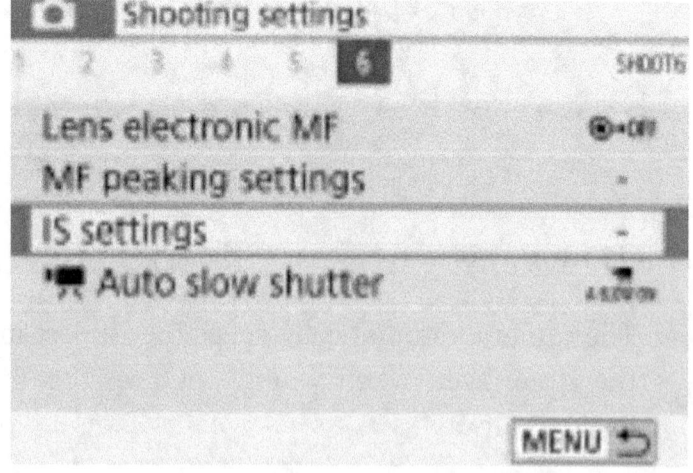

2. Choose "Digital IS."

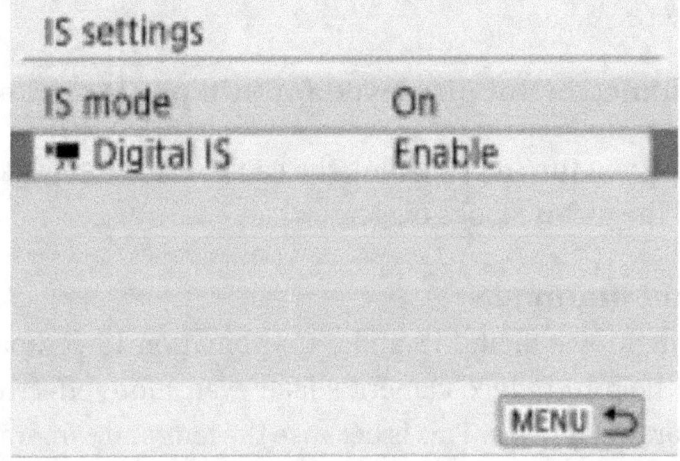

3. Pick a setting that works best for you.

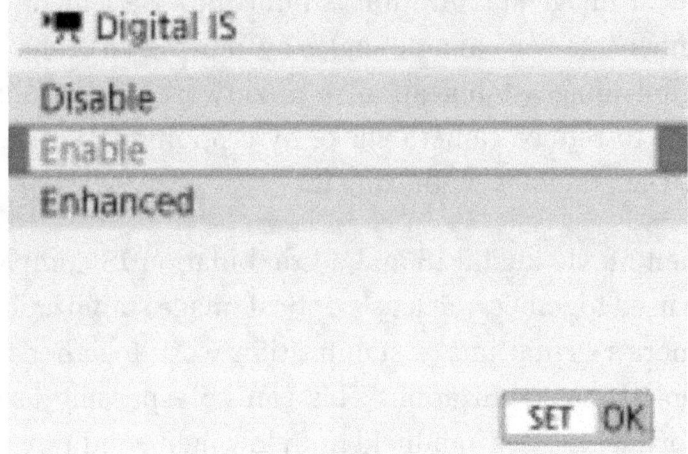

Disable

Movie digital IS, which helps stabilize videos, is turned off.

Enable

The shaky camera effect will be fixed, and the picture will be larger.

Enhanced (Not displayed for still photos shooting.)

When you turn on [Enable], the camera shake gets fixed better, and the picture looks bigger.

Combination IS

Using Movie digital IS and a Combination IS-compatible lens will help to reduce camera shake even more effectively when recording movies. This is because the lens and camera will work together to stabilize the image.

Optical image stabilization is built into the lens and helps to compensate for camera shake by moving the lens elements. Digital image stabilization is a software-based solution that helps to reduce camera shake by cropping the image slightly and then digitally stabilizing it.

When Movie digital IS and a Combination IS-compatible lens are used together, the lens's optical image stabilization and the camera's digital image stabilization work together to provide even better stabilization. This can be especially useful when recording movies handheld or in low light conditions.

Note:

1. Movie digital IS doesn't work if your lens doesn't have an Image Stabilizer or if the IS switch is turned off. If you

specify [Enable] or [Enhanced], the Movie digital IS icon blinks.

2. If your lens has a focal length longer than 800 mm, the Movie digital IS won't work with it.

3. The Movie digital IS might not work as well with certain video recording sizes.

4. The wider your camera's view is (like a wide-angle shot), the better the image stabilization will be. But if you're zoomed in (telephoto), the stabilization won't work as effectively.

5. If you're using a tripod, it's a good idea to turn off Movie digital IS.

6. Depending on what you're filming and the conditions, you might notice some blurriness or the subject momentarily looking out of focus because of the Movie digital IS.

7. If you're using a TS-E lens, fish-eye lens, or a non-Canon lens, it's recommended to disable Movie digital IS.

8. Movie digital IS can make the image look grainy and you might see noise or dots of light..

Cautions for Movie Recording

1. Don't point the camera at really bright lights like the sun or strong artificial lights. It could harm the camera's parts.

2. If you film something with a lot of details, you might see extra or wrong colors in the video.

3. If you use certain settings and the camera's settings change while recording a video, the colors might look different.

4. When you film under fluorescent or LED lights, the video might look like it's flickering.

5. If you focus the camera during video recording in low light, you might get some strange lines in the video. This can happen with certain lenses too.

6. It's better to test recording with zooming before making your actual video. Zooming while recording might cause problems like changes in brightness or strange sounds.

7. Using a very large aperture setting might make it hard for the camera to focus quickly.

8. While recording a video, if you use autofocus, you might notice the focus changing suddenly, the video getting brighter or pausing, and you could hear the lens moving.

9. Don't cover the camera's built-in microphones with your fingers or anything else.

10. Make sure to set the date, time, and time zone for the camera to work correctly in different temperatures.

11. If you see a message saying "Overheated! Shutting down," turn off the camera and wait for at least 3 minutes. If you're recording a 4K video or a high frame rate video, wait for at least 9 minutes. The actual recording times might be shorter depending on the conditions.

Compression and Frame Rates

Compression

IPB (Standard)

It uses IPB compression to record movies. It efficiently compresses several frames together during recording.

ALL-I

ALL-I compression compresses each frame of a time-lapse video individually. This results in larger file sizes than IPB compression, but it also makes the videos easier to edit. When you edit a time-lapse video that is compressed with ALL-I, you can easily remove or add frames without affecting the quality of the video. This is because each frame is compressed independently.

Frame Rate (fps: frame per second)

119.88fps/ 59.94fps/ 29.97fps

In places like North America, Japan, South Korea, and Mexico, where the TV system is NTSC.

100.00fps/50.00fps/25.00fps

For places like Europe, Russia, China, and Australia they use the PAL TV system.

23.98fps

It means you can use a frame rate of 23.98 frames per second (fps) for movies, specifically when the video system is set to NTSC.

High Frame Rate

You can shoot high-quality movies in slow motion with this camera. Just enable the High Frame Rate option, and you can record movies at either 119.88 frames per second or 100.00 frames per second.

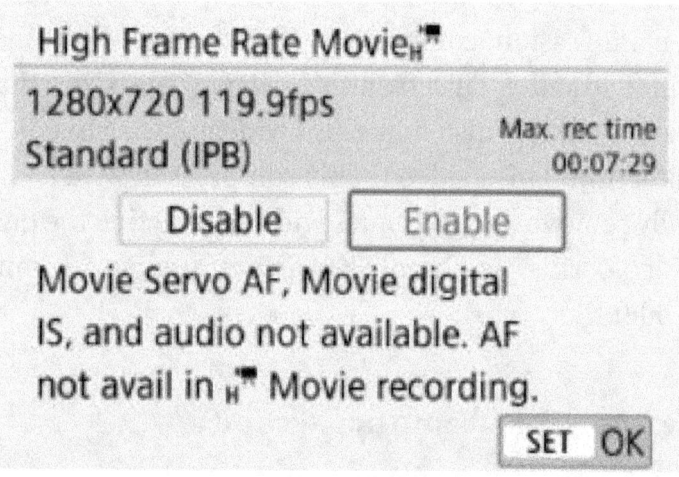

These movies are perfect for slow-motion playback. Each movie can be up to 7 minutes and 29 seconds long. When you play these movies, they appear in slow motion at 1/4 of their original speed because they are recorded at 29.97 frames per second or 25.00 frames per second.

Note: Make sure to turn off the "Movie rec. size" setting. If you record fast videos in certain lighting, the screen might flicker. Also, when you start or stop recording, the video might freeze briefly. And the frame rates displayed on the screen won't match the video frame rate. Sound was not captured or saved.

CONCLUSION

The Canon EOS M200 is a compact and lightweight mirrorless interchangeable lens camera (MILC) that is perfect for beginners and hobbyists alike. It features a 24.1MP APS-C sensor, a DIGIC 8 image processor, and a variety of easy-to-use features that make it easy to capture high-quality photos and videos.

The Canon EOS M200 User Guide is a comprehensive and informative resource for users of all levels of experience. It covers everything from the basics of camera operation to more advanced topics such as creative shooting techniques and troubleshooting.

The book begins with an introduction to the camera and its features, followed by a detailed guide to each of the camera's menus and settings. It then goes on to cover more specific topics such as shooting modes, exposure control, focusing, and white balance.

The book also includes a number of helpful tips and tricks, such as how to get the best results in different shooting conditions and how to use the camera's creative features. It also provides a troubleshooting section that addresses some of the most common problems that users may encounter.

The Canon EOS M200 User Guide is an excellent resource for anyone who wants to learn more about their camera and how to use it to take great photos. It is well-written and easy to understand, and it covers a wide range of topics in a comprehensive and informative way.

www.ingramcontent.com/pod-product-compliance
Lightning Source LLC
Chambersburg PA
CBHW072212290526
45794CB00004B/1727